OUTWITTING
THE DEVIL

ORIGINAL 1938 CLASSIC

OUTWITTING THE DEVIL

NAPOLEON HILL

WITH STUDY GUIDE
BY THERESA PUSKAR

Published 2025 by Gildan Media LLC
aka G&D Media
www.GandDmedia.com

OUTWITTING THE DEVIL. Copyright © 2025 by G&D Media.

No part of this book may be reproduced or transmitted in any form, by any means, (electronic, photocopying, recording, or otherwise) without the prior written permission of the author. No liability is assumed with respect to the use of the information contained within. Although every precaution has been taken, the author and publisher assume no liability for errors or omissions. Neither is any liability assumed for damages resulting from the use of the information contained herein.

Front Cover design by David Rheinhardt of Pyrographx

Interior design by Meghan Day Healey of Story Horse, LLC

Library of Congress Cataloging-in-Publication Data is available upon request

ISBN: 978-1-7225-0721-3

10 9 8 7 6 5 4 3 2 1

Contents

Study Guide Introduction 7

Chapter 1: My First Meeting with Andrew Carnegie 13

Chapter 2: A New World Is Revealed to Me 37

Chapter 3: A Strange Interview with the Devil 52

Chapter 4: Drifting with the Devil 69

Chapter 5: The Confession Continues 98

Chapter 6: Hypnotic Rhythm 121

Chapter 7: Seeds of Fear 139

Chapter 8: Definiteness of Purpose 147

Chapter 9: Education and Religion 158

Chapter 10: Self-Discipline 184

Chapter 11: Learning from Adversity 201

Chapter 12: Environment, Time, Harmony and Caution 218

Summary 240

The Secret Chapter: My Invisible Counselors 246

Rebuilding Character Through Auto-Suggestion 256

Study Guide Introduction

When I was first asked to write this study guide, I was intrigued, perplexed, and excited. While I am familiar with Neale Donald Walsch's bestseller, *Conversations with God*, I had no idea that almost sixty years prior, one of the preliminary authors of the self-help movement had written about a similar conversation, only with God's archnemesis.

WHY THIS BOOK AND WHY NOW?

In chapter 2 of *Outwitting the Devil*, Napoleon Hill writes, "The whole world is undergoing a change of such stupendous proportions that millions of people have become panic-stricken with worry, doubt, indecision, and fear! It seems to me that now is a splendid time for those who have come to the cross-roads of doubt to endeavor to become acquainted with their 'other selves.'" I had to pause for a moment and reread the original date of this publication. Yes, it was, in fact, 1938. Yet, those words so aptly expressed the state of Americans today. While Napoleon Hill's book was written over eighty years ago, it is very applicable today.

I was intrigued that this task was being asked of me at this time. I believe that this is a very important era in the evolution of humankind. I think that we are at a precipice, a tipping point, to coin a phrase from Malcolm Gladwell's brilliant book. The best analogies that I can give are twofold. First, I liken the polarized social, economic, cultural, religious, and political climates that exist today in America to cancer. If we don't know we have the disease, we cannot cure it. Similarly, the ugly finger-pointing, and angry lashing out that we see throughout America today is a cancer. At least we know it exists. If we see it, then we can respond to it and potentially cure it. It all comes down to choice.

TO CONTINUE THE FIGHT OR TO LEAP?

Second, I see the world at a pivotal tipping point. As an analogy, we are at the edge of a massive cliff. In the ocean of cause and effect directly beneath us, there are jagged rocks and treacherous waters. However, beyond that rocky, deadly terrain are calmer waters of possibilities. We are at a decision point. In our angry righteousness, as we righteously yield to no one, we can either push each other off the cliff's edge into the sharp, deadly boulders below, or we can all take a long, extended dive into the unknown but clearly calmer waters beyond. To dive, we must be willing to build a better relationship first and foremost with ourselves.

We must do our internal work. We have to be willing to look into the recesses of our minds and hearts, challenging our current beliefs as victims, underdogs, and pawns and take ownership for the thoughts we think, the actions we take, and the choices we make. To do so takes great courage and a willingness to remove the masks of whom we project ourselves to be to the world. We must dig deep and be authentic and honest with ourselves about ourselves. Then and only then can this world start to heal. Again, it all comes down to choice.

A DIALOGUE WITH SATAN?

To be frank, while I was raised as a Christian, throughout my life I have struggled with believing in an actual being known as the Devil. So, I thought that writing a study guide in response to a conversation with the Devil was going to be a difficult undertaking. However, as I read through the pages, I realized that whether you believe in a Devil or not, does not really matter. I think we can all agree that there are both positive and negative forces in this world—energies that have great power over our hearts, minds, and actions. What matters is not the perceived form and lack thereof of negativity, but more how we can observe it, engage with it, and learn from it.

In this book, *Outwitting the Devil*, Napoleon Hill does a magnificent job of dialoguing with the Devil (negativity), learning of its apparent traps and tricks so that we can each face its manipulations honestly and squarely. We can then look within ourselves and take the necessary steps toward growth as the self-aware human beings that we are all capable of becoming.

SOME PERCEPTIONS ARE DATED

I have to say that some of the statements shared in this text are more than just dated. They can be construed as downright offensive. For example, the Devil describes the so-called ways in which women influence men through injecting softness by using "cooing baby tones into their voices" and by "closing their eyes into a half-closed position which registers hypnotism."

When I first read it, I was offended by the incredibly patriarchal example given. However, if you can step back and look for the learning opportunity in this statement, you may be able to move past it. It could be translated to the statement that "whatever means you use (whatever your gender may be), take an inventory of how you manipulate others through flattery." The bottom line is that, while some of the statements are dated and would frankly not be tolerated if it were written for today's audience, I am glad that I looked into the deeper universal meaning, and I didn't throw out the baby with the bathwater.

HOW TO PERCEIVE POLITICAL STATEMENTS

Napoleon Hill also makes comments in the book that reference past US presidents and the choices they made. He clearly has a position and a great deal to say about social welfare programs, the churches, schooling, unemployment, entrepreneurialism, and the like. For example, at one point in the book, according to the Devil, "millions of boys are preparing Americans to become Hitlerized. They intend to take over the country 'with ballots instead of bullets.'" He continues by stating that he does this by "stirring up strife between employers and employees."

He further claims that the president will Hitlerize America by turning the government against business and industry. He asserts that "when propaganda has done its work thoroughly, one of my boys will move in as a dictator and the Nine Old Men on your Supreme Court with their silly notions of the Constitution will move out! Everyone will be given a job or fed from the government treasury. When men's bellies are filled, they drift freely with one who does the filling."

I would encourage you to sit with these and other statements. If they trouble you, then you have an opportunity to take a deeper dive into your psyche. You may be able to learn why it commands such a strong response in you. While I can't speak for you, I know that when my buttons are really pushed, usually there is something in the statement that I don't want to own within myself, some resistance.

SUGGESTIONS FOR AN OPTIMAL EXPERIENCE

Before you begin reading, please find a pen and a notebook that you can use to respond to the study guide questions. It is important that you have something to write in as you read, so that you can capture insights and innovations in the moment that they arise. When we wait, we very often forget them.

For several of the questions, I asked you to rate yourself in a particular area of your life on a scale from 1 to 10. In your notebook, you need not re-create the scales. Simply list the number that best reflects your current state.

Most importantly, I created the study guide to support your own personal evolutionary process. I encourage you to respond to the study guide questions that correspond to the contents at the end of each chapter. While you may be tempted to first read the book, and then revisit the study guide afterward, you may not get back to completing it. Doing the study guide in tandem with the book will support deeper comprehension and integration of these masterful principles into your life. It will transform your experience from one of passivity to one of actionable transformation.

I firmly believe that as each of us does our own personal growth work, we affect the consciousness of the masses. By taking proactive steps in your life based on insights and wisdom that Napoleon Hill shares in this book, you will not only raise your consciousness, but also that of humankind.

Theresa Puskar
Study Guide Author

Chapter 1

My First Meeting with Andrew Carnegie

For more than a quarter of a century my major purpose has been that of isolating and organizing into a philosophy of achievement the causes of both failure and success, with the object of being helpful to others who have neither the inclination nor the opportunity to engage in this form of research.

My labor began in 1908, as the result of an interview that I had with the late Andrew Carnegie. I frankly told Mr. Carnegie that I wished to enter law school and that I had conceived the idea of paying my way through school by interviewing successful men and women, finding out how they came by their success, and writing stories of my discoveries for magazines. At the end of our first visit Mr. Carnegie asked whether or not I possessed enough courage to carry out a suggestion he wished to offer me. I replied that courage was about all I did have and that I was prepared to do my best to carry out any suggestion he cared to offer.

He then said, "Your idea of writing stories about men and women who are successful is commendable, as far as it goes, and I have no intention of trying to discourage you from carrying out your purpose, but I must tell you that if you wish to be of enduring service, not only to those now living, but to posterity as well, you can do so if you will take the time to organize all of the causes of failure as well as all of the causes of success.

"There are millions of people in the world who have not the slightest conception of the causes of success and failure. The schools and colleges teach practically everything except the principles of individual achievement. They require young men and women to spend from four to eight years acquiring abstract knowledge, but do not teach them what to do with this knowledge after they get it.

"The world is in need of a practical, understandable philosophy of achievement, organized from the factual knowledge gained from the experience of men and women in the great university of life. In the entire field of philosophy I find nothing which even remotely resembles the sort of philosophy which I have in mind. We have few philosophers who are capable of teaching men and women the art of living.

"It seems to me that here is an opportunity which should challenge an ambitious young man of your type; but ambition alone is not enough for this task which I have suggested. The one who undertakes it must have courage and tenacity.

"The job will require at least twenty years of continuous effort, during which the one who undertakes it will have to earn his living from some other source, because this sort of research is never profitable at the outset, and generally those who have contributed to civilization through work of this nature have had to wait a hundred years or so after their own funerals to receive recognition for their labor.

"If you undertake this job, you should interview not only the few who have succeeded, but the many who have failed. You should carefully analyze many thousands of people who have been classed as 'failures,' and I mean by the term 'failures,' men and women who come to the closing chapter of life disappointed because they did not attain the goal which they had set their hearts upon achieving. As inconsistent as it may seem, you will learn more about how to succeed from the failures than you will from the so-called successes. They will teach you what not to do.

"Along toward the end of your labor, if you carry it through successfully, you will make a discovery which may be a great surprise to you. You will discover that the cause of success is not something separate and apart from the man; that it is a force so intangible in nature that the majority of men never recognize it; a force which might be properly called the 'other self.' Noteworthy is the fact that this 'other self' seldom exerts its influence or makes itself known excepting at times of unusual emergency, when men are forced, through adversity and temporary defeat, to change their habits and to think their way out of difficulty.

"My experience has taught me that a man is never quite so near success as when that which he calls 'failure' has overtaken him, for it is on occasions of this sort that he is forced to think. If he thinks accurately, and with persistence, he discovers that so-called failure usually is nothing more than a signal to re-arm himself with a new plan or purpose. Most real failures are due to limitations which men set up in their own minds. If they had the courage to go one step further, they would discover their error."

BEGIN LIFE ANEW

Mr. Carnegie's speech reshaped my entire life and planted in my mind a burning purpose, which has driven me ceaselessly, and this despite the fact that I had but a vague idea as to what he meant by the term "other self."

During my labor of research into the causes of failure and success I have had the privilege of analyzing more than 25,000 men and women who were rated as "failures," and over 500 who were classed as "successful." Many years ago I caught my first glimpse of that "other self" Mr. Carnegie had mentioned. The discovery came, as he said it would, as the result of two major turning-points of my life, which constituted emergencies that forced me to think my way out of difficulties such as I had never before experienced.

I wish it were possible to describe this discovery without the use of the personal pronoun, but this is impossible because it came through personal experiences from which it cannot be separated. To give you the complete picture I shall have to go back to the first of these two major turning-points and bring you up to the discovery step by step.

The research necessary for the accumulation of the data, from which the seventeen principles of achievement and the thirty major causes of failure were organized, required years of labor.

I had reached the false conclusion that my task of organizing a complete philosophy of personal achievement had been completed. Far from having been completed, my work had merely begun. I had erected the skeleton of a philosophy by organizing the seventeen principles of achievement and the thirty major causes of failure, but that skeleton had to be covered with the flesh of application and experience. Moreover, it had to be given a soul through which it might inspire men and women to meet obstacles without going down under them.

The "soul," which had yet to be added, as I discovered later, became available only after my "other self" made its appearance, through two major turning-points of my life.

Resolving to turn my attention, and whatever talents I might possess, into monetary returns through business and professional channels, I decided to go into the profession of advertising, and I became the advertising manager of the LaSalle Extension University of Chicago. Everything went along beautifully for one year, at the end of which I was seized by a violent dislike for my job and resigned.

I then entered the chain store business, with the former president of the LaSalle Extension University, and became the president of the Betsy Ross Candy Company. Unfortunate—or what seemed to me at the time to be unfortunate—disagreements with business associates disengaged me from that undertaking.

The lure of advertising still was in my blood, and I tried again to give expression to it by organizing a school of advertising and salesmanship, as a part of Bryant & Stratton Business College.

The enterprise was sailing smoothly and we were making money rapidly when the United States entered World War I. In response to an inner urge which no words can describe, I walked away from the school and entered the service of the United States government, under President Woodrow Wilson's personal direction, leaving a perfectly sound business to disintegrate.

On Armistice Day 1918, I began the publication of *The Golden Rule* magazine. Despite the fact that I did not have a penny of capital, the magazine grew rapidly and soon gained a nation-wide circulation of nearly half a million, ending its first year's business with a profit of $3,156.

Some years later I learned, from an experienced publisher, that no man experienced in the publication and distribution of national magazines would think of starting such a magazine with less than half a million dollars of capital.

The Golden Rule magazine and I were destined to part company. The more we succeeded the more discontented I became, until finally, due to an accumulation of petty annoyances caused by business associates, I made them a present of the magazine and stepped out. Through that move perhaps I tossed a small fortune over my shoulder.

Next I organized a training school for salesmen. My first assignment was to train a sales army of 3,000 people for a chain store company, for which I received $10 for each salesman who went through my classes. Within six months my work had netted me a little over $30,000. Success, as far as money was concerned, was crowning my efforts with abundance. Again I became "fidgety" inside. I was not happy. It became more obvious every day that no amount of money would ever make me happy.

Without the slightest reasonable excuse for my actions, I stepped out and gave up a business from which I might easily have earned a healthy salary. My friends and business associates thought I was crazy, and they were not backward about saying so.

Frankly, I was inclined to agree with them, but there seemed nothing I could do about it. I was seeking happiness and I had not found it. At least that is the only explanation I could offer for my unusual actions. What man really knows himself?

That was during the late fall of 1923. I found myself stranded in Columbus, Ohio, without funds, and worse still, without a plan by which to work my way out of my difficulty. It was the first time in my life that I had actually been stranded because of lack of funds.

Many times previously I had found money to be rather shy, but never before had I failed to get what I needed for my personal conveniences. The experience stunned me. I seemed totally at sea as to what I could or should do.

I thought of a dozen plans by which I might solve my problem, but dismissed them all as being either impractical or impossible of achievement. I felt like one who was lost in a jungle without a compass. Every attempt I made to work my way out brought me back to the original starting point.

For nearly two months I suffered with the worst of all human ailments: indecision. I knew the seventeen principles of personal achievement, but what I did not know was how to apply them! Without knowing it I was facing one of those emergencies of life through which, Mr. Carnegie had told me, men sometimes discover their "other selves."

My distress was so great that it never occurred to me to sit down and analyze its cause and seek its cure.

DEFEAT IS CONVERTED INTO VICTORY

One afternoon I reached a decision through which I found the way out of my difficulty. I had a feeling that I wanted to get out into the "open spaces" of the country, where I could get a breath of fresh air and think.

I began to walk, and had gone seven or eight miles when I felt myself brought suddenly to a standstill. For several minutes I stood there as if I had been glued to my tracks. Everything around me went dark. I could hear the loud sound of some form of energy which was vibrating at a very high rate.

Then my nerves became quiet, my muscles relaxed, and a great calmness came over me. The atmosphere began to clear, and as it did so, I received a command from within which came in the form of a thought, as near as I can describe it.

The command was so clear and distinct that I could not misunderstand it.

In substance it said, "The time has come for you to complete the philosophy of achievement which you began at Carnegie's suggestion. Go back home at once and begin transferring the data you have gathered from your own mind to written manuscripts." My "other self" had awakened.

For a few minutes I was frightened. The experience was unlike any I had ever undergone before. I turned and walked rapidly until I reached home. As I approached the house, I saw my three little boys looking out of a window of our house at our neighbor's children, who were dressing a Christmas tree in the house next door.

Then I recalled that it was Christmas Eve. Moreover, I recalled, with a feeling of deep distress such as I had never known before, that there would be no Christmas tree at our house. The look of disappointment on the faces of my children reminded me painfully of that fact.

I went into the house, sat down at my typewriter, and began at once to reduce to writing the discoveries I had made concerning the causes of success and failure. As I placed the first sheet of paper in the typewriter I was interrupted by that same strange feeling which had come over me out in the country a few hours before, and this thought flashed into my mind:

"Your mission in life is to complete the world's first philosophy of individual achievement. You have been trying in vain to escape your task, each effort having brought you failure. You are seeking happiness. Learn this lesson, once and forever, that you will find happiness only by helping others to find it! You have been a stubborn student. You had to be cured of your stubbornness through disappointment. Within a few years from now the whole world will start through an experience which will place millions of people in need of the philosophy which you have been directed to complete. Your big opportunity to find happiness by rendering useful service will have come. Go to work, and do not stop until you have completed and published the manuscripts which you have begun."

I was conscious of having arrived, at last, at the end of life's rainbow, and I was happy!

DOUBT MAKES ITS APPEARANCE

The "spell," if the experience may be so called, passed away. I began to write. Shortly thereafter my "reason" suggested to me that I was embarking upon a fool's mission. The idea of a man who was down and almost out presuming to write a philosophy of personal achievement seemed so ludicrous that I laughed hilariously, perhaps scornfully.

I squirmed in my chair, ran my fingers through my hair, and tried to create an alibi that would justify me in my own mind in taking the sheet of paper out of my typewriter before I had really begun to write, but the urge to continue was stronger than the desire to quit. I became reconciled to my task and went ahead.

Looking backward now, in the light of all that has happened, I can see that those minor experiences of adversity through which I had passed were among the most fortunate and profitable of all of my experiences. They were blessings in disguise because they forced me to continue a work which finally brought me an opportunity to make myself more useful to the world than I might have been had I succeeded in any previous plan or purpose.

For almost three months I worked on those manuscripts, completing them during the early part of 1924. As soon as they had been completed, I felt myself again being lured by the desire to get back into the great American game of business.

Succumbing to the lure, I purchased the Metropolitan Business College in Cleveland, Ohio, and began to lay plans for increasing its capacity. By the end of 1924 we had developed and expanded, by adding new courses, until we were doing a business nearly double the best previous record the school had ever known.

Again the germ of discontentment began to make itself felt in my blood. Again I knew that I could not find happiness in that sort of endeavor. I turned the business over to my associates and went on the lecture platform, lecturing on the philosophy of achievement, to the organization of which I had devoted so many of my previous years.

One night I was booked to lecture in Canton, Ohio. Fate, or whatever it is that seems sometimes to shape the destiny of men, no matter how hard they may try to battle against it, again stepped into the picture and brought me face to face with a painful experience.

In my Canton audience sat Don R. Mellett, publisher of the *Canton Daily News*. Mr. Mellett became so thoroughly interested in the philosophy of individual achievement on which I lectured that night that he invited me to come to see him the following day.

That visit resulted in a partnership agreement which was to have taken place on the first of the following January when Mr. Mellett planned to resign as publisher of the *Daily News*, to take charge of the business and publishing of the philosophy on which I had been working.

However, in July 1926, Mr. Mellett was murdered by Pat McDermott, an underworld character, and a Canton, Ohio, policeman, both of whom were sentenced to life imprisonment. He was murdered because he was exposing in his newspaper a hook-up between the bootleggers and certain members of the Canton police force. The crime was one of the most shocking that the prohibition era produced.

CHANCE (?) SAVES MY LIFE

The morning after Mr. Mellett's death I was called on the telephone and put on notice, by some unknown person, that I had one hour in which to get out of Canton; that I could go voluntarily within the hour, but if I waited longer I probably would go in a pine box. My business association with Mr. Mellett had apparently been misunderstood. His murderers evidently believed I was directly connected with the exposé he was making in his newspapers.

I did not wait for the one hour time limit to expire, but immediately got into my automobile and drove down to the home of relatives in the mountains of West Virginia, where I remained until the murderers had been placed in jail.

That experience came well within the category described by Mr. Carnegie as an "emergency" that forces men to think. For the first time in my life I knew the pain of constant fear. My experience of a few years before, in Columbus, had filled my mind with doubt and temporary indecision, but this one had filled it with a fear which I seemed unable to remove. During the time that I was in hiding I seldom left the house at night, and when I did step out I kept my hand on an automatic pistol in my coat pocket, with the safety catch unlatched for immediate action. If a strange automobile stopped in front of the house where I was hiding, I went into the basement and carefully scrutinized its occupants through the basement windows.

After some months of this sort of experience, my nerves began to crack. My courage had completely left me. The ambition which had heartened me during the long years of labor in my search for the causes of failure and success also had departed.

Slowly, step by step, I felt myself slipping into a state of lethargy from which I was afraid I should never be able to emerge. The feeling must have been closely akin to that experienced by one who suddenly steps into quicksand and realizes that every effort to extricate himself carries him just so much deeper. Fear is a self-generating morass.

If the seed of insanity had been in my make-up, surely it would have germinated during those months of living death. Foolish indecision, irresolute dreams, doubt and fear were my mind's concern, day and night.

The "emergency" I faced was disastrous in two ways. First, the very nature of it kept me in a constant state of indecision and fear.

Secondly, the forced concealment kept me in idleness, with its attendant heaviness of time, which I naturally devoted to worry.

My reasoning faculty had almost been paralyzed. I realized that I had to work myself out of this state of mind. But how? The resourcefulness which had helped me to meet all previous emergencies seemed to have completely taken wing, leaving me helpless.

Out of my difficulties, which were burdensome enough up to this point, grew another which seemed more painful than all the others combined. It was the realization that I had spent the better portion of my past years in chasing a rainbow, searching hither and yon for the causes of success, and finding myself now more helpless than any of the 25,000 people whom I had judged as being "failures."

This thought was almost maddening. Moreover, it was extremely humiliating, because I had been lecturing all over the country, in schools and colleges and before business organizations, presuming to tell other people how to apply the seventeen principles of success, while here I was, unable to apply them myself. I was sure that I never could again face the world with a feeling of confidence.

Every time I looked at myself in a mirror I noticed an expression of self-contempt on my face, and not infrequently I did say things to the man in the mirror which are not printable. I had begun to place myself in the category of charlatans who offer others a remedy for failure which they themselves cannot successfully apply.

The criminals who had murdered Mr. Mellett had been tried and sent to the penitentiary for life; therefore, it was perfectly safe, as far as they were concerned, for me to come out of hiding and again take up my work. I could not come out, however, because now I faced circumstances more frightful than the criminals who had sent me into hiding.

The experience had destroyed whatever initiative I had possessed. I felt myself in the clutches of some depressing influence which seemed like a nightmare. I was alive; I could move around, but I could not think of a single move by which I might continue to seek the goal which I had, at Mr. Carnegie's suggestion, set for myself. I was rapidly becoming indifferent, not only toward myself, but worse still, I was becoming grouchy and irritable toward those who had given me shelter during my "emergency."

I faced the greatest emergency of my life. Unless you have gone through a similar experience, you cannot possibly know how I felt. Such experiences cannot be described. To be understood they must be felt.

THE MOST DRAMATIC MOMENT OF MY LIFE

The turn came suddenly, in fall 1927, more than a year after the Canton incident. I left the house one night and walked up to the public school building, on top of a hill above the town.

I had reached a decision to fight the matter out with myself before that night ended. I began to walk around the building, trying to force my befuddled brain to think clearly. I must have made several hundred trips around the building before anything which even remotely resembled organized thought began to take place in my mind. As I walked I repeated over and over to myself, "There is a way out and I am going to find it before I go back to the house." I must have repeated that sentence a thousand times.

Moreover, I meant exactly what I was saying. I was thoroughly disgusted with myself, but I entertained a hope of salvation.

Then like a flash of lightning out of a clear sky, an idea burst into my mind with such force that the impulse drove my blood up and down my veins:

"This is your testing time. You have been reduced to poverty and humiliated in order that you might be forced to discover your 'other self.'"

For the first time in years I recalled what Mr. Carnegie had said about this "other self." I recalled now that he said I would discover it toward the end of my labor of research into the causes of failure and success, and that the discovery usually came as the result of an emergency, when men are forced to change their habits and to think their way out of difficulty.

I continued to walk around the schoolhouse, but now I was walking on air. Subconsciously I seemed to know that I was about to be released from the self-made prison into which I had cast myself.

I realized that this great emergency had brought me an opportunity, not merely to discover my "other self," but to test the soundness of the philosophy of achievement which I had been teaching others as being workable. Soon I would know whether it would work or not. I made up my mind that if it did not work I would burn the manuscripts I had written and never again be guilty of telling other people that they were "the masters of their fate, the captains of their souls."

The full moon was just rising over the mountain top. I had never seen it shine so brightly before. As I stood gazing at it, another thought flashed into my mind. It was this:

"You have been telling other people how to master fear and how to surmount the difficulties which arise out of the emergencies of life. From now on you can speak with authority because you are about to rise above your own difficulties with courage and purpose, resolute and unafraid."

With that thought came a change in the chemistry of my being which lifted me into a state of exultation I had never before known. My brain began to clear itself of the state of lethargy into which it had lapsed. My faculty of reason began to work once more.

For a brief moment I was happy to have had the privilege of going through those long months of torment, because the experience provided an opportunity for me to test the soundness of the principles of achievement which I had so laboriously wrested from my research.

When this thought came to me, I stopped still, drew my feet closely together, saluted (I did not know what or whom), and stood rigidly at attention for several minutes. This seemed, at first, like a foolish thing to do, but while I was standing there another thought came through in the form of an "order" that was as brief and snappy as any ever given by a military commander to a subordinate.

The order said, "Tomorrow get into your automobile and drive to Philadelphia, where you will receive aid in publishing your philosophy of achievement."

There was no further explanation and no modification of the order. As soon as I received it, I walked back to the house, went to bed, and slept with peace of mind such as I had not known for over a year.

When I awoke the following morning, I got out of bed and immediately began to pack my clothes and make ready for the trip to Philadelphia. My reason told me that I was embarking upon a fool's mission. Who did I know in Philadelphia to whom I might apply for financial aid in publishing eight volumes of books at a cost of $25,000? I asked myself.

Instantly the answer to that question flashed into my mind, as plainly as if it had been uttered in audible words: "You are following orders now, instead of asking questions. Your 'other self' will be in charge during this trip."

There was another condition which seemed to make my preparation to go to Philadelphia absurd. I had no money!

This thought had barely occurred to me when my "other self" exploded it by giving another sharp order, saying, "Ask your brother-in-law for fifty dollars and he will lend it to you."

The order seemed definite and final. Without further hesitation I followed instructions. When I asked my brother-in-law for the money, he said, "Why, certainly you can have fifty dollars, but if you are going to be gone very long you had better take a hundred dollars." I thanked him and said I thought fifty dollars would be enough. I knew it was not enough, but that was the amount my "other self" had commanded me to ask for and that is the amount I secured.

I was greatly relieved when I found that my brother-in-law was not going to ask me why I was going to Philadelphia. If he had known all that had taken place in my mind during the previous night, he perhaps would have thought I should go to a psychiatric hospital for treatment instead of going to Philadelphia on a wild-goose chase.

MY "OTHER SELF" TAKES COMMAND

I left with my head telling me I was a fool and my "other self" commanding me to ignore the challenge and carry out my instructions.

I drove all night, arriving in Philadelphia the next morning. My first thought was to look up a modestly priced boarding house where I could rent a room for about one dollar a day.

Here again my "other self" took charge and gave the command to register at the most exclusive hotel in the city. With a little more than forty dollars of my remaining capital in my pocket, it seemed like financial suicide when I marched up to the desk and asked for a room; or rather I should say I started to ask for a room when my newly discovered "other self" gave the order to ask for a suite of rooms, the cost of which would about consume my remaining capital in two days. I obeyed.

The bell-boy picked up my bags, handed me my claim check for my automobile, and bowed me toward the elevator as if I were the Prince of Wales. It was the first time in more than a year that any human being had shown me such deference. My own relatives, with whom I had been living, far from having shown me deference, had (so I imagined) felt I was a burden on their hands, and I am sure that I was, because no man in the frame of mind that I had been in for the past year could be anything other than a burden to all with whom he came into contact.

It was becoming apparent that my "other self" was determined to wean me away from the inferiority complex which I had developed.

I tossed the bell-boy a dollar. I started to estimate what my hotel bill would be by the end of the week when my "other self" commanded me to get my mind entirely off of all thoughts of limitation, and to conduct myself, for the time being, just as I would if I had all the money I wanted in my pockets.

The experience I was passing through was both new and strange to me. I had never posed as being anything other than what I believed myself to be.

For nearly half an hour this "other self" gave orders which I followed to the letter during the subsequent period of my stay in Philadelphia. The instructions were given through the medium of thoughts which presented themselves in my mind with such force that they were readily distinguishable from my ordinary self-created thoughts.

I RECEIVE STRANGE "ORDERS" FROM A STRANGE SOURCE

My instructions began in this fashion:

> "You are now completely in charge of your 'other self.' You are entitled to know that two entities occupy your body, as in fact two similar entities occupy the body of each living person on earth.
>
> "One of these entities is motivated by and responds to the impulse of fear. The other is motivated by and responds to the impulse of faith. For more than a year you have been driven, like a slave, by the fear entity.
>
> "Night before last the faith entity gained control over your physical body, and you are now motivated by that entity. For the sake of convenience you may call this faith entity your 'other self.' It knows no limitations, has no fears, and recognizes no such word as 'impossible.'
>
> "You were directed to select this environment of luxury, in a good hotel, as a means of discouraging the return to power of the fear entity. That fear-motivated 'old self' is not dead; it has merely been dethroned. And it will follow you around wherever you go, awaiting a favorable opportunity to step in and take charge of you again. It can gain control of you only through your thoughts. Remember this, and keep the doors to your mind tightly closed against all thoughts which seek to limit you in any manner whatsoever, and you will be safe.
>
> "Do not permit yourself to worry about the money you will need for your immediate expenses. That will come to you by the time you must have it.

"Now, let us get down to business. First of all you should know that the faith entity now in charge of your body performs no miracles, nor does it work in opposition to any of nature's laws. As long as it is in charge of your body it will guide you when you call on it, through impulses of thought which it will place in your mind, in carrying out your plans through the most logical and convenient natural media available.

"Above everything else, get this fact clearly fixed in your mind, that your 'other self' will not do your work for you; it will only guide you intelligently in achieving for yourself the objects of your desires.

"This 'other self' will aid you in translating your plans into reality. Moreover, you should know that it begins, always, with your major, or most pronounced desire. At this time your major desire—the one which brought you here—is to publish and distribute the results of your research into the causes of success and failure. You estimate that you will need approximately $25,000.

"Among your acquaintances there is a man who will supply you with this needed capital. Begin, at once, to call into your mind the names of all persons of your acquaintance whom you have reason to believe might be induced to furnish the financial aid you require.

"When the name of the logical person comes into your mind, you will recognize it immediately. Communicate with that person and the aid you seek will be given. In your approach, however, present your request in terminology such as you would use in the usual course of business transactions. Make no reference whatsoever to this introduction you have had to your 'other self.' If you violate these instructions, you will meet with temporary defeat.

"Your 'other self' will remain in charge and continue to direct you as long as you rely upon it. Keep doubt and fear and worry, and all thoughts of limitation, entirely out of your mind.

"That will be all for the present. You will now begin to move of your own free will, precisely as you did before you discovered your 'other self.' Physically you are the same as you have always been; therefore, no one will recognize that any change has taken place in you."

I looked around the room, blinked my eyes, and to make sure that I was not dreaming, I got up and walked over to a mirror and looked at myself closely. The expression on my face had changed from one of doubt to one of courage and faith. There was no longer any doubt in my mind that my physical body was in charge of an influence far different from the one which had been dethroned two nights before, as I walked around that schoolhouse in West Virginia.

STUDY GUIDE

Chapter 1:
My First Meeting with Andrew Carnegie

1. Napoleon Hill opens this book by sharing the contents of conversation that he had with Andrew Carnegie early in his career. He emphasizes how that message greatly impacted the rest of his life. Write a list of the individuals you have met in your lifetime who have made an impact on the trajectory of your life. Make note of what they said and how they impacted you.

2. Are there any books that you have read, movies you have seen, or conferences you have attended that impacted who you are today and what choices you have made in your life? List them and describe what steps you have taken in response to the messages you received.

3. Often predicaments we find ourselves in or experiences we have had can also change the trajectory of our lives. Do a review of your life, scanning each year from your birth to present day. List the key personal experiences you have had that had a great impact on you. What decisions and choices have you made in response to them?

4. Now that you have listed the experiences or communications that have impacted you, reflect on whether they supported your successes or failures.

5. Did you learn and evolve after experiencing the difficult situations? If so, please explain how. If not, why do you think you have not?

6. Are there any negative feelings that continue to haunt you in response to any difficult experiences you had? Please explain.

7. Andrew Carnegie stated that there is much more to learn from those who struggled with "failure" over those who celebrated success. Take a moment to reflect on situations in which you felt you failed. What did you learn? In retrospect, are you grateful for those experiences or do you still feel regret?

8. Carnegie emphasized that Napoleon needed to have "courage and tenacity" to spend at least twenty years on this pursuit, and that he would not be recognized for his efforts until "a hundred years or so" after his funeral. How do you think you might respond, if you were told that your life's work would not be recognized during your lifetime? Would you be willing to continue it knowing this?

9. To date, what do you believe your contributions have been toward your personal evolution and the evolution of those whom you have touched in your life?

10. Carnegie asserted that Napoleon "will make a discovery which may be a great surprise to you. You will discover that the cause of success is not something separate and apart from the man; that it is a force so intangible in nature that the majority of men never recognize it; a force which might be properly called the 'other self.'" What do you believe he was referencing?

11. Do you experience an "other self" in your life? Please explain.

12. Carnegie stated that "man is never quite so near success as when that which he calls 'failure' has overtaken him." Have you ever found yourself feeling overcome with disappointment and hopelessness, and just at that time, your luck shifted? If so, please explain.

13. Carnegie continued by sharing that "most real failures are due to limitations which men set up in their own minds." Are there any limitations that you are currently setting up in your own mind? Please list them and then commit to further exploring them as you continue to read this book and respond to the study guide.

14. Reflect on your life. Is there anyone with whom you had a poignant conversation that greatly impacted you and, as such, changed your life? If so, please describe it.

15. In further reflection, have you ever spoken to an individual or group where you thought that your message was impactful in their lives? If so, please explain.

16. If you did not discover any way in which you impacted the lives of others, set an intention to have your impact be revealed to you. While you may not be consciously aware, you have impacted others in your life. By setting an intention for this to be revealed to you, in time, trust that it will.

Begin Life Anew

17. Do you currently have a "burning purpose" in your life, like that of Napoleon Hill as he described his feelings after talking to Dale Carnegie?

18. If you are currently not aware of a "burning purpose" in your life, would you like to feel that passionate about something? If so, what might that be? One way to pose this question to your subconscious is by asking yourself, "If I were to die tomorrow, what message would I like to leave the world?"

19. Napoleon Hill revealed that his discovery of his "other self" came through two personal experiences or major turning points that he had in his life. Write a list of at least three turning points you experienced in your life.

20. Napoleon found himself on several career paths in which he could not find happiness. In each situation, he left the unhappy position. Have you ever found yourself in a similar circumstance? If so, as you reflect, were you able to leave the situation, or did you find yourself staying longer than you think you should have? Please explain.

21. In the fall of 1923, Napoleon found himself stuck in a situation where he was without a plan nor funds with which he could work his way out of the difficulty he was in. Have you ever felt yourself in this situation? What did you do?

22. Napoleon poses the question, "What man really knows himself?" in response to the choices he makes to leave positions that he is not happy with but make him money. Do you believe that you "know" yourself? Please explain.

23. Napoleon shared that he suffered from indecision for nearly two months. Have you ever found yourself paralyzed and struggling with indecision? In retrospect, do you know why you felt stuck? How did you eventually move through the situation?

24. The first step that Napoleon took to convert defeat into victory was to get outside and walk outdoors. Have you ever tried this technique? If not, what do you do to pull out of negativity?

25. He was told by his "other self" to go back to the suggestion that Dale Carnegie made to him. His first reaction was fear. Have you ever found yourself listening to a message or a voice in your head that seems to be beyond your own? If so, what was your response?

26. Napoleon received a message that he will only find happiness by helping others find their own happiness. He was advised to get back to completing the manuscript on failure and success, that the world will need it. Based on that message, he found himself feeling happy again. Have you ever focused your energy on making others happy? If so, did you find yourself feeling better? If not, why not?

27. Spend one day focusing all your energy on making others happy. Then at the end of the day, make note of how you feel.

Doubt Makes Its Appearance

28. Napoleon Hill speaks of how the "spell" of his conversation with his "other self" passed away after a time. Have you experienced enthusiasm after inspiration dying within you? What did you do to re-inspire yourself into action?

29. In retrospect, Napoleon saw the minor experiences of adversity as being "the most fortunate and profitable" of all his experiences. Reflect on your life. Can you think of a challenging experience that, in retrospect, benefited you? If so, please explain. If not, write about an adverse experience and contemplate how it may have been a blessing in disguise. Write about any insights you have.

30. The author thought that he would find happiness through his success in doubling the occupancy of the Metropolitan Business College after purchasing it, but he soon felt discontent creeping back into his psyche. Have you ever noted yourself achieving a goal, only to find that your sense of joy was short-lived soon after? Please explain.

31. Napoleon shares the shocking story of how his life was in jeopardy after the murder of his new business partner, Mr. Mellett. He referred to his "near miss in death" experience as "an 'emergency' that forces men to think." He stated that for the first time in his life, he knew the pain of constant fear. On a scale from 1 to 10, how fearful do you believe yourself to be?

1 —— 2 —— 3 —— 4 —— 5 —— 6 —— 7 —— 8 —— 9 —— 10

32. Napoleon found himself eventually slipping into a state of deeper fear and lethargy. Have you ever found yourself in such a state—emotionally paralyzed and unable to pull yourself out? Describe the state and what you believed was the precursor.

33. In that state, the author found himself consumed with worry. Do you sometimes find yourself consumed with worry? Write a list of all the items that you currently worry about.

34. Now that you have your list, do an estimate on what percentage of your energy you expend each day with worry.

35. He also suffered from indecisiveness and the ability to reason. Have you ever been in such a state. Describe your feelings and see if you can sense where you were holding these feelings in your physical body. You may have experienced them in your heart area, or solar plexus/gut, your neck or shoulders.

36. Napoleon Hill eventually experienced feelings of self-contempt, as he felt hypocritical, lecturing on success and feeling more of a failure than those he had written about. Have you felt hypocritical in your life? If so, please explain.

The Most Dramatic Moment of My Life

37. At the point in which an attitude shift was made, Napoleon Hill continued to repeat a mantra to himself, "There is a way out and I'm going to find it before I go back to the house." Do you ever use mantras (repeated positive messaging)? If so, did you find this practice effective? Why or why not?

38. On that hilltop, Napoleon Hill got a message that he was being tested to discover his "other self." He recalled that the learning would come in a response to a life emergency, when he was forced to change his habits. Reflect and recall a time in your life when you were "forced" to change your habits. Write about the experience, especially the events that led up to the change.

39. It is said that we best teach that which we first needed to experience and learn ourselves. Write a list of experiences you have had in your life that you eventually used to teach others.

40. He received an order, "Tomorrow get in your automobile and drive to Philadelphia, where you will receive aid in publishing your philosophy of achievement." Have you ever experienced such a thought—a command that felt strong and important? If so, please explain.

41. Napoleon Hill got an insight that he was following orders from his "other self" as opposed to asking questions. Have you ever felt compelled by a strong message that seemed to have come from outside of yourself? If so, did you follow the guidance? Please explain.

42. Napoleon felt that his "other self" was working toward weaning him away from the inferiority complex he had been feeling. He was compelled to let go of limiting thoughts and act as if he had all the money that he wanted in his pockets. Take five minutes to close your eyes

and envision your life as if you were not experiencing limitations in any way. Write about your experience.

I Receive Strange "Orders" from a Strange Source

43. Napoleon Hill is instructed that "two entities occupy the body of each living person on earth." One is motivated and responds to fear, and the other by faith. Take a moment to check in with your mind and body. Which do you feel currently has a louder voice in your psyche? How do you know this is so?

44. He was instructed that the fear-self was not dead but had been dethroned. It awaits favorable opportunities to step in and take over. What situations or mindsets do you think create such opportunities for fear to run your life? For example, do you believe your greatest challenges are in your career, relationships, or physical health?

45. Napoleon was guided not to worry about the money he would need for his immediate expenses—that it would come to him by the time he must have it. Do you think you could respond as he did if in a similar circumstance? Please explain.

46. Napoleon makes it clear that the "other self" will not do your work for you. It will only guide you. Take a moment and close your eyes. Take three deep breaths and quiet your mind. Then ask your "other self" if there are any messages that you currently should hear. If you receive any, write them down immediately. If not, set an intention to get guidance and have faith that the messages will be revealed.

47. In the previous exercise, if you received a strong, clear message that enlisted excitement within you and is for your highest good and the highest good of others, it may be a powerful first step to follow through on that message. If you choose to do so, be sure to journal on your experience.

48. In the end, Napoleon looked in the mirror and saw a change from doubt to courage and faith in his expression. He looked the same on the outside, but he experienced a vast change from within. If you haven't already done so, give yourself time to get quiet and listen to your "other self"—that strong, supportive voice within your mind. Write down any ideas or insights you have. If you cannot focus, that's okay. Fully embrace that without judgment and write about your experience with lacking focus. With a strong intent to better your life, whatever arises within you is perfect on your road to continued personal growth.

Chapter 2

A New World Is Revealed to Me

Obviously I had undergone a new birth by which I had been separated from all forms of fear. I now had courage such as I never before had experienced. Despite the fact that I had not as yet been shown how, or from what source, I would be able to secure the necessary funds which I was seeking, I had such absolute faith that the money would be forthcoming that I could see it already in my possession.

On but few occasions in my entire life have I experienced such faith. It was a feeling which one person cannot describe to another. There are no words in the English language suitable for such a description—a fact that all who have had similar experiences can easily verify.

I proceeded immediately to carry out the instructions I had received. All feeling that I had embarked upon an impossible mission had now left me. One by one I began to call into my mind the names of all my acquaintances I knew to be financially able to supply me with the $25,000 which I needed, starting with the name of Henry Ford, and going over the entire list of more than three hundred people. My "other self" plainly said, "Keep on searching."

THE DARKEST HOUR IS JUST BEFORE DAWN

But I had come to the end of my rope. My entire list of acquaintances had been exhausted, and with it my physical endurance as well. I had been at work, concentrating my mind upon that list of names, for the better part of two days and nights, having stopped only long enough to sleep for a few hours.

I leaned back in my chair, shut my eyes, and went into a sort of doze for a few minutes. I was aroused by what seemed to be an explosion in the room. As I regained consciousness the name of Albert L. Pelton came into my mind . . . and with it a plan which I knew instantly to be the plan through which I would succeed in getting Mr. Pelton to publish my books. I remembered Mr. Pelton only as an advertiser in *The Golden Rule* magazine, which I had formerly published. I sent for a typewriter, addressed a letter to Mr. Pelton at Meriden, Connecticut, and described the plan just as it had been handed over to me. He answered by telegram, saying that he would be in Philadelphia to see me the following day.

When he came I showed him the original manuscripts of my philosophy, and briefly explained what I believed its mission to be. He turned through the pages of the manuscripts for a few minutes, then stopped suddenly and fixed his eyes on the wall for a few seconds and said, "I will publish your books for you."

The contract was drawn; a substantial advance payment on royalties was given me, the manuscripts were turned over to him, and he took them back to Meriden.

I did not ask him at the time what caused him to reach a decision to publish my books before he had read the manuscripts, but I do know that he supplied the necessary capital, printed the books, and assisted me in selling many thousands of sets of them to his own clientele of book buyers, who were located in practically every English-speaking country in the world.

MY "OTHER SELF" MAKES GOOD

Three months from the day that Mr. Pelton called on me in Philadelphia, a completed set of my books was placed on the table in front of me, and my income from the sale of the books began to run high enough for all my needs. These books are now in the hands of my students all over the world.

My first royalty check from the sale of my books was for $850. As I opened the envelope in which it came, my "other self" said, "Your only limitation is the one which you set up in your own mind!"

I am not sure that I understand just what this "other self" is, but I do know that there can be no permanent defeat for the man or the woman who discovers it and relies upon it.

The day after Mr. Pelton came to see me in Philadelphia, my "other self" presented me with an idea which solved my immediate financial problem. The idea flashed into my mind that automobile merchandising methods had to undergo a drastic change and that future salesmen in this field would have to learn to sell automobiles instead of merely serving as buyers of used car trade-ins, as most of them were doing at the time.

It also occurred to me that young men who had just finished college and who, therefore, knew nothing of the old "tricks" of automobile merchandising would be the material out of which this new brand of salesmen could best be developed.

The idea was so distinct and impressive that I immediately called the sales manager of the General Motors Company on long-distance telephone and briefly explained my plan to him. He too was impressed by it and referred me to the West Philadelphia branch of the Buick Automobile Company, which was then owned and managed by Earl Powell. I went to see Mr. Powell, explained my plan to him, and he retained me at once to train fifteen carefully selected young college men through whom the plan was put into operation.

My income from that retainer was more than enough to take care of all of my expenses for the following three months, until the returns from the sale of my books began to come in, including the cost of that expensive suite of rooms, over which I had at first been so concerned.

My "other self" had not disappointed me. The money I needed was in my hands at the proper time, just as I had been assured the money would be. By this time I had been convinced that my trip to Philadelphia was by no means a fool's mission, as my reason had indicated it would be before I left West Virginia.

From that time right up to this very minute everything I have needed has come to me, and this despite the fact that the whole world has recently passed through a period of economic depression, when the bare necessities of life have not always been available to all people. Sometimes the arrival of the material things I needed has been a little late, but I can truthfully say that my "other self" has always met me at the crossroads when I have come to them, and indicated which path I should follow.

The "other self" follows no precedents, recognizes no limitations, and always finds a way to accomplish desired ends! It may meet with temporary defeat, but not with permanent failure. I am as sure of the soundness of this statement as I am of the fact of being engaged in writing these lines.

Meanwhile, I earnestly hope that some of the millions of men and women who have been wounded by the business depression and other unpleasant experiences will discover within themselves this strange entity which I have called my "other self," and that the discovery will lead them, as it has led me, into a closer relationship with that source of power which surmounts obstacles and masters difficulties, instead of being mastered by them. There is a great power to be discovered in your "other self"! Search sincerely and you will find it.

"FAILURE": A BLESSING IN DISGUISE

I have made another discovery as the result of this introduction to my "other self," namely, that there is a solution for every legitimate problem, no matter how difficult the problem may seem.

I have also discovered that there comes with every experience of temporary defeat, and every failure and every form of adversity, the seed of an equivalent benefit.

Mind you, I did not say the full-blown flower of success, but the seed from which that flower may be made to germinate and grow. I know of no exception to this rule. The seed of which I speak may not always be observed, but you may be sure it is there, in one form or another.

I do not pretend to understand all about this strange force which reduced me to poverty and want, and filled me with fear, and then gave me a new birth of faith through which I have been privileged to extend help to tens of thousands who found themselves slipping. But I do know that such a force has come into my life and that I am doing all I can to place others in communication with it.

During my quarter-century of research into the causes of success and failure I have discovered many principles of truth which have been helpful to me and to others, but nothing I have observed has impressed me more than the discovery that every great leader of the past, whose record I have examined, was beset by difficulties and met with temporary defeat before "arriving."

From Christ on down to Edison, the men who have achieved most have been those who met with the most stubborn forms of temporary defeat. This would seem to justify the conclusion that Infinite Intelligence has a plan, or a law, by which it hurdles men over many obstacles before giving them the privilege of leadership or the opportunity to render useful service in a noteworthy fashion.

I would not wish to be again subjected to the experiences through which I passed during that fateful Christmas Eve in 1923, and since, on that eventful evening when I walked around the school house in West Virginia and fought that terrible battle with fear, but all the wealth in the world would not induce me to divest myself of the knowledge I have gained from those experiences.

FAITH HAS A NEW MEANING TO ME

I repeat that I do not know exactly what this "other self" is, but I know enough about it to lean upon it in a spirit of absolute faith in times of difficulty, when the ordinary reasoning faculty of my mind seems to be inadequate for my needs.

The economic depression which started in 1929 brought misery to millions of people, but let us not forget that the experience also brought many blessings, not the least of these being the knowledge that there is something infinitely worse than being forced to work. It is being forced not to work. In the main, that depression was more of a blessing than it was a curse, if analyzed in the light of the changes it brought to the minds of those who were wounded by it. The same is true of every experience which changes men's habits and forces them to turn to the great "within" for the solution of their problems. The time which I spent in seclusion in West Virginia was, by great odds, the most severe punishment of my life, but the experience brought blessings in the form of needed knowledge which more than offset the suffering which it cost me. These two results—the suffering and the knowledge gained from it—were inevitable. The law of compensation, which Emerson so clearly defined, made this result both natural and necessary.

What the future may hold for me in the way of disappointment, through temporary defeat, I of course have no way of knowing. I do know, however, that no experience of the future can possibly wound me as deeply as have some of those of the past, because I am now on speaking terms at least with my "other self."

Since this "other self" took charge of me, I have come by useful knowledge which I am sure I never would have discovered while my old fear entity was on the throne. For one thing I have learned that those who meet with difficulties which seem insurmountable may, if they will do so, best overcome these difficulties by forgetting them for a time and helping others who have greater problems.

THE VALUE OF GIVING BEFORE TRYING TO GET

I am sure that no effort which we extend to those who are in distress can go without some form of adequate reward. Not always does the reward come from those to whom the service is rendered, but it will come from one source or another.

I seriously doubt that any man can avail himself of the benefits of his "other self" as long as he is steeped in greed and avarice, envy and fear, but if I am wrong in this conclusion then I still have the unusual honor of being one who has found peace of mind and happiness through a viewpoint that was not sound. I would prefer being thus wrong and happy, to being right and unhappy! But this viewpoint is not wrong!

As long as I remain on good terms with my "other self" I shall be able to acquire every material thing that I need. Moreover, I shall be able to find happiness and peace of mind. What more could anyone else accomplish?

The sole motive which inspired me to write this book was a sincere desire to be helpful to others by sharing with them as much as they may be prepared to accept of the stupendous fortune which became mine the moment I discovered my "other self." This fortune, happily, is one that cannot be measured in material or financial terms alone, because it is greater than everything which such things represent.

Material and financial fortunes, when reduced to their most liquid terms, are measurable in terms of bank balances. Bank balances are no stronger than banks. This other fortune of which I speak is measurable, not only in terms of peace of mind and contentment but as manifested in those adept at prayer.

My "other self" has taught me to concentrate upon my purpose and to forget about the plan by which it is to be attained when I go to prayer. I am not suggesting that material objects may be acquired without plans. What I am saying is that the power which translates one's thoughts or desires into realities has its source in an Infinite Intelligence which knows more about plans than the one doing the praying.

Stating the case in another way, may it not be wise, when praying, to trust to the Universal Mind to hand over the plan best suited for the attainment of the object of that prayer? My experience with prayer has taught me that so often all which results from prayer is a plan (if the prayer is answered at all), a plan that is suited for the attainment of the object of the prayer through natural and material media. The plan must be transmuted, through self-effort action.

I know nothing about any form of prayer which can be induced to work favorably in a mind that is colored, in the slightest degree, by fear.

A NEW WAY TO PRAY

Since becoming better acquainted with my "other self," my way of praying is different from what it was before. I used to go to prayer only when facing difficulty. Now I go to prayer before difficulty overtakes me, when possible. I now pray, not for more of this world's goods and greater blessings, but to be worthy of that which I already have. I find that this plan is better than the old one.

Infinite Intelligence seems not at all offended when I give thanks and show that I am grateful for the blessings which have crowned my efforts. I was astounded, when I first tried this plan of offering a prayer of thanks for what I already possessed, to discover what a vast fortune I had owned without being appreciative of it.

For example, I discovered that I possessed a sound body which had never been seriously damaged by illness. I had a mind which was reasonably well balanced. I had a creative imagination through which

I could render useful service to great numbers of people. I was blessed with all the freedom I desired, in both body and mind. I possessed an imperishable desire to help others who were less fortunate.

I discovered that happiness, the highest aim of mankind, was mine for the taking, business depression or no business depression.

Last, but by no means least, I discovered that I had the privilege of approaching Infinite Intelligence, either for the purpose of offering thanks for what I already possessed, or to ask for more, and for guidance.

It may be helpful for every reader of this book to take inventory of his or her intangible assets. Such an inventory may disclose possessions of priceless value.

SOME SIGNS WE HAVE OVERLOOKED

The whole world is undergoing a change of such stupendous proportions that millions of people have become panic-stricken with worry, doubt, indecision, and fear! It seems to me that now is a splendid time for those who have come to the crossroads of doubt to endeavor to become acquainted with their "other selves."

All who wish to do so will find it helpful if they take a lesson from nature. Observation will show that the eternal stars shine nightly in their accustomed places; that the sun continues to send down its rays of warmth, causing Mother Earth to yield an over-abundance of food and clothing; that water continues to flow downhill; that the birds of the air and the wild animals of the forest receive their accustomed requirements of food; that useful day follows restful night; that busy summer follows the inactive winter; that the seasons come and go precisely as they did before the 1929 depression began; that, in reality, only men's minds have ceased to function normally, and this, because men have filled their minds with fear.

Observation of these simple facts of everyday life may be helpful as a starting point for those who wish to supplant fear by faith.

I am not a prophet, but I can, with all due modesty, predict that every individual has the power to change his or her material or financial status by first changing the nature of his or her beliefs.

Do not confuse the word "belief" with the word "wish." The two are not the same. Everyone is capable of "wishing" for financial, material, or spiritual advantages, but the element of faith is the only sure power by which a wish may be translated into a belief, and a belief into reality.

And right here is an appropriate place at which to call attention to a real benefit which anyone may experience by deliberately using faith in focusing attention upon any form of constructive desire. The mind acts upon one's dominating, or most pronounced desires. There is no escape from this fact. It is a fact indeed. "Be careful what you set your heart upon, for it surely shall be yours."

FAITH IS THE BEGINNING OF ALL GREAT ACHIEVEMENT

If Edison had stopped by merely wishing for the secret with which electric energy might be harnessed and made to serve through the incandescent lamp, that convenience to civilization would have remained among nature's multifarious secrets. He met with temporary defeat more than 10,000 times before wresting this secret from nature. It was finally yielded up to him because he believed it would be, and he kept on trying until he had the answer.

Edison uncovered more of nature's secrets (they might have been called "miracles" at an earlier period) in the realm of physics than did any other man who ever lived, and this because he became acquainted with his "other self." I have his own word for this, but even if I did not have it, his achievements of themselves have disclosed the secret in their unfoldment.

Nothing within reason is impossible to the man who knows and relies upon his "other self." Whatever man believes to be true has a way of becoming true.

A prayer is a released thought, sometimes expressed in audible words and at other times expressed silently. I have observed by experience that a silent prayer is as efficacious as the one which is expressed in words. I have observed also that one's state of mind is the determining factor when prayer works, as well as when it does not.

My conception of the "other self" which I have tried to describe is that it merely symbolizes a newly discovered approach to Infinite Intelligence, an approach which one may control and direct through the simple process of mixing faith with one's thoughts. This is only another way of saying that I now have greater faith in the power of prayer.

The state of mind known as faith apparently opens to one the medium of a sixth sense through which one may communicate with sources of power and information far surpassing any available through the five physical senses.

There comes to your aid, and to do your bidding, with the development of the sixth sense, a strange power which, let us assume, is a guardian angel who can open to you at all times the door to the Temple of Wisdom. The "sixth sense" comes as near to being a miracle as anything I have ever experienced, and it appears so perhaps because I do not understand the method by which this principle is operated.

This much I do know—that there is a power or a first cause, or an Intelligence which permeates every atom of matter, and embraces every unit of energy perceptible to man; that this Infinite Intelligence converts acorns into oak trees, causes water to flow downhill in response to the law of gravity, follows night with day, and winter with summer, each maintaining its proper place and relationship to the other. This Intelligence may aid in transmuting one's desires into concrete or material form. I have this knowledge because I have experimented with it and have experienced it.

I have for many years followed the habit of taking personal inventory of myself once a year, for the purpose of determining how many of my weaknesses I have bridged or eliminated, and to ascertain what progress, if any, I had made during the year.

STUDY GUIDE

Chapter 2:
A New World Is Revealed to Me

1. Napoleon Hill opens this chapter by sharing that he had undergone a "new birth" where he had been separated from all forms of fear. Has there ever been a time where you felt totally fearless in your life? If so, describe it in as much detail as possible.

2. When did you feel the greatest amount of faith in your life? Please explain.

3. Were you able to sustain your faith for a prolonged period? Why or why not?

The Darkest Hour Is Just Before Dawn

4. Right when Napoleon Hill had come to the end of his rope as he searched for financial backing for his book, suddenly the name "Albert L. Pelton" came to mind. He followed the impulse and came to a publishing agreement with Mr. Pelton. Have you ever been in a situation with which you had just given up hope, and in that moment, you had a breakthrough? If so, please describe the event.

My "Other Self" Makes Good

5. After receiving his first check from the sale of his books, Napoleon Hill's "other self" stated, "Your only limitation is the one which you set up in your own mind!" Do you believe that you alone create the limitations in your life? Please explain.

6. Napoleon Hill emphasizes that "there can be no permanent defeat" for the man or woman who discovers the "other self." Do you believe this to be true? Do you have any such experience in your life? If so, please explain.

7. The "other self" gave Napoleon an insight that he could train men who were new college graduates how to sell cars, and in doing so, he could solve his immediate financial problems. Have you ever had

such a solution come to you in a flash? If so, please explain. If not, set an intention to pay attention to that inner voice and anticipate such a message. Once experienced, write about it.

8. Napoleon stated that the "other self" always guided him when he was at crossroads and indicated which path he should follow. While it may have met with temporary defeat, it never navigated him into permanent failure. Ultimately it guided him toward a deeper connection with the source of all creation. Have you ever experienced a force that created such a connection in your life? If so, please explain. If not, what do you think may be blocking the connection?

"Failure": A Blessing in Disguise

9. Through these experiences, Napoleon discovered that there is a solution to every problem, no matter how difficult. Do you believe this to be true? Why or why not?

10. He also states that from every diversity there is the seed of an equivalent benefit. Reflect on your life. Was there a time when you noted an adversity later revealed as a learning opportunity or positive outcome? If so, please explain.

11. Napoleon states that every great leader of the past, whose record he had examined, "was beset by difficulties and met with temporary defeat before 'arriving.'" Do some research and write about at least one such leader who first faced adversity and apparent defeat before circumstances changed. Write about your findings.

Faith Has a New Meaning to Me

12. Napoleon talks of leaning on that "other self" when his mind seems to be inadequate. Have you ever perceived your mind to be inadequate?

13. According to Napoleon Hill, being forced not to work is infinitely worse than being forced to work. Have you ever found yourself in such a situation? If you, do you find this statement to be true?

14. Napoleon references Emerson's law of compensation when he reflects on the two results he experienced. Research this law and write about how it applies to your life.

The Value of Giving Before Trying to Get

15. Napoleon opens this segment of the book stating that he'd rather be wrong and happy instead of being right and unhappy. What are your thoughts on this statement and how it pertains to your belief system?

16. He asserts that if he remains in good terms with his "other self," he will be able to find peace and happiness and acquire all the material things that he needs. Do you have such faith about your life? Please explain.

17. Napoleon states that he wrote this book to help others. Write a list of the ways in which you feel called to help others.

18. Napoleon asserts that we should concentrate more on our purpose and less on how we might do so. Do you know what your purpose is? Do you think you can let go of the "how" in your endeavors?

19. Answers to our prayers are transmuted through self-effort and action; prayer alone is not the answer. Do you believe this to be true? Why or why not?

20. He further asserts that fear interferes with prayer's ability to work. Have you experienced this in your life? Please explain.

A New Way to Pray

21. Napoleon shares that the way he prays has differed since this experience. His new prayers are toward being worthy of what he already has (as opposed to praying for more worldly goods and blessings). How do you currently pray? Do you believe your current prayers to be effective? Why or why not?

22. Napoleon encourages you to take an inventory of your intangible assets. Take some time now to list all that you have and experience in your life for which you are grateful. Be sure to list all, big and small.

Some Signs We Have Overlooked

23. This book was originally published in 1938. Napoleon Hill speaks of a world that is riddled with worry, doubt, indecision, and fear. On a scale from 1 to 10, rate how much you believe the world is currently filled with these emotions.

    1 —— 2 —— 3 —— 4 —— 5 —— 6 —— 7 —— 8 —— 9 —— 10

24. Napoleon speaks of how Mother Nature's world continues to function with consistency and flow. He suggests that observing such simple facts of everyday life can be a good starting point for those who wish to shift from fear to faith. Do you currently find solace in observing the rhythms of nature? Why or why not?

25. You can change your beliefs and, in doing so, you can change your life. You are cautioned, however, not to replace the word "belief" with the word "wish." Why do you believe Napoleon Hill sets a distinction between the two? Please explain.

26. "Be careful what you set your heart upon, for it surely shall be yours." Give an example in your life where you may have wished upon something that was not fully in your best interest, only to find yourself in a quagmire.

Faith Is the Beginning of All Great Achievement

27. Napoleon Hill attributes Edison's success with the light bulb to his perseverance and to his connection with his "other self." Write about at least one other innovator that you believe paralleled such success.

28. Napoleon Hill shares that he believes in the power of prayer. Do you? Why or why not?

29. Prayer is described as a "released thought"—a mixing of faith with one's thoughts. How might you define prayer?

30. Have you ever prayed? If so, when and why? What were the circumstances that led you to prayer?

31. Do you believe in the "sixth sense"? Why or why not?

32. Napoleon Hill shares that he does a personal inventory each year to ascertain how many of his weaknesses he has overcome throughout the year. Reflect on the past year and write a list of those challenges you have overcome through the year.

33. In reviewing your list, note what you attribute your successes to. Do you believe that Infinite Intelligence played a role? Please explain.

Chapter 3

A Strange Interview with the Devil

While you are reading the interview with the Devil, you will recognize from the brief description I have given you of the history of my life what a desperate effort the Devil made to muzzle me before I gained public recognition. You will understand also, after reading the interview with the Devil, why the interview had to be preceded by this personal history of my background.

Before you begin to read the interview, I want you to have a clear picture of the final fling the Devil had at me, and be it remembered with profit that it was this final fling which gave mercy a chance to turn and twist the Devil's tail until he squealed out his confession.

The Devil's undoing began with the depression in 1929. Through that fortunate turn of the Wheel of Life, I lost my 600-acre estate in the Catskill Mountains; my income was entirely cut off; the Harriman National Bank, in which all my funds were deposited, folded up and was wiped out. Before I realized what was happening, I found myself caught up in a spiritual and economic hurricane which evolved into a worldwide catastrophe of such force that no individual or group of individuals could withstand it.

While waiting for the storm to cease and the stampede of human fear to stop, I moved to Washington, D.C., the city from which I made my start after my first meeting with Andrew Carnegie, nearly a quarter of a century previously.

There seemed nothing for me to do except sit down and wait. All I had was time. After three years of waiting without tangible results, my restless soul began to push me back into service.

There was little opportunity for me to teach a philosophy of success when the world around me was in the midst of abject failure, and men's minds were filled with the fear of poverty.

This thought came to me one evening while I was sitting in my automobile, in front of the Lincoln Memorial on the Potomac River, within the shadow of the Capitol. With it came another thought: The world had staged an unprecedented depression over which no human being had control. With that depression had come to me an opportunity to test the philosophy of self-determination, to the organization of which I had devoted the better portion of my adult life. Once more I had the opportunity to learn whether my philosophy was practical or mere theory.

I realized too the opportunity had come to test a claim I had made hundreds of times that "every adversity brings with it the seed of an equivalent advantage." What, if any, I asked myself, were the advantages to me of a world depression?

When I began to look for a direction in which I might move to test my philosophy, I made the most shocking discovery of my life. I discovered that through some strange power which I did not understand, I had lost my courage; my initiative had been demoralized; my enthusiasm had been weakened. Worst of all, I was sorely ashamed to acknowledge that I was the author of a philosophy of self-determination, because down deep in my heart I knew, or thought I knew, that I could not make my philosophy pull me out of the hole of despair in which I found myself.

While I floundered in a state of mental bewilderment, the Devil must have been dancing a jig of rejoicing. At last he had "the author of the world's first philosophy of individual achievement" pinned under his thumb and paralyzed with indecision.

But the Devil's opposition must have been at work too!

* * * * * * * * * * * * * *

As I sat there in front of the Lincoln Memorial, reviewing in retrospect the circumstances which had so many times previously lifted me to great heights of achievement, only to let me drop to equal depths of despair, a happy thought was handed over to me in the form of a definite plan of action by which I believed I could throw off that hypnotic feeling of indifference with which I had been bound.

In the interview with the Devil, the exact nature of the power by which I had been deprived of my initiative and courage has been described. It is the same power with which millions of others were bound during the Great Depression. It is the chief weapon with which the Devil ensnares and controls human beings.

The sum and substance of this thought which came to me was this: Despite the fact that I had learned from Andrew Carnegie and more than five hundred others of equal business and professional achievements that noteworthy achievements in all walks of life come through the application of the Master Mind (the harmonious coordination of two or more minds working to a definite end), I had failed to make such an alliance for the purpose of carrying out my plan to take the philosophy of individual achievement to the world.

Despite the fact I had understood the power of the Master Mind, I had neglected to appropriate and use this power. I had been laboring as a "lone wolf" instead of allying myself with other and superior minds.

AN ANALYSIS

Let us now briefly analyze the strange interview you are about to begin. Some who read will want to ask, after they finish it, "Did you really interview the Devil, or did you merely interview an imaginary Devil?" Some may wish the answer to this question before they begin the interview.

I will answer in the only truthful way I could answer... by saying that the Devil I interviewed may have been real, just as he claimed to be, or he may have been the creation of my own imagination. Whichever he was, whether real or imaginary, is of little importance compared with the nature of the information conveyed through the interview.

The important question is this: Does the interview convey dependable information which may be helpful to people who are trying to find their places in the world? If it conveys that sort of information, no matter whether it is conveyed in the form of fact or fiction, then it is worthy of serious analysis through careful reading. I am not concerned in the least as to the real source of the information or as to the real nature of the Devil whose astounding story you are about to read. I am concerned only with the fact that the Devil's confession squares perfectly with what I have seen of life.

I believe the interview does convey information of practical benefit to all who have not found life to be friendly, and the reason I believe so is the fact that I have made the central theme of this book yield to me all the happiness I need, in the form best suited to my nature.

I have had experience with enough of the principles mentioned by the Devil to assure me that they will do exactly what he says they will. That is enough for me. So I pass the story of the interview on to you for whatever you may be able to make it pay in useful dividends.

Perhaps you will get the greatest values if you accept the Devil as being what he claims himself to be, relying upon his message for whatever it may bring you that you can use, and not worrying as to who the Devil is or whether he exists.

If you want my honest personal opinion, I believe the Devil is exactly who he claims to be. Now let us analyze his strange confession.

After forcing his way into the consciousness of the Devil, "Mr. Earthbound" began the unwilling interview with questions which could not be evaded...

HERE BEGINS THE INTERVIEW WITH THE DEVIL

Q. I have uncovered the secret code by which I can pick up your thoughts. I have come to ask you some very plain questions. I demand that you give me direct and truthful answers. Are you ready for the interview, Mr. Devil?

A. Yes, I am ready, but you must address me with more respect. During this interview you will address me as "Your Majesty."

Q. By what right do you demand such royal respect?

A. You should know I control 98 percent of the people of your world. Do you not think that entitles me to rate as royalty?

Q. Have you proof of your claim?

A. Yes, plenty of it.

Q. Of what does your proof consist?

A. Of many things. If you want answers, you will address me as "Your Majesty." Some things you will understand; some you will not. In order that you may get my viewpoint, I shall describe myself and correct the false notions people have of me and my place of abode.

Q. That is a fine idea, Your Majesty. Start by telling me where you live. Then describe your physical appearance.

A. My physical appearance? Why, my dear Mr. Earthbound, I have no physical body. I would be handicapped by such an encumbrance as those in which you earthbound creatures live. I consist of negative energy, and I live in the minds of people who fear me. I also occupy one half of every atom of physical matter and every unit of mental and physical energy. Perhaps you will better understand my nature if I tell you I am the negative portion of the atom.

Q Oh, I see what you are preparing to claim. You are laying the foundation to say that if it were not for you, there would be no world, no stars, no electrons, no atoms, no human beings, nothing. Is that correct?

A. True! Absolutely true.

Q Well, if you only occupy one half of energy and matter, who occupies the other half?

A. The other half is occupied by my opposition.

Q Opposition? What do you mean?

A. The opposition is what you earthbound call God.

Q So you have the universe divided up with God. Is that your claim?

A. Not my claim, but the actual fact. Before this interview is finished you will understand why my claim is true. You will also understand why it has to be true, or there could be no world such as yours, no earthbound creatures such as you. I am no beast with a forked tongue and a spiked tail.

Q But you do control the minds of 98 out of every 100 people. You said so yourself. Who causes all the misery in this 98 percent Devil-controlled world, if you do not?

A. I have not said that I do not cause all the misery of the world. On the other hand, I boast of it. It is my business to represent the negative side of everything, including the thoughts of you earthbound people. How else could I control people? My opposition controls positive thought. I control negative thought.

Q How do you gain control of the minds of people?

A. Oh, that is easy: I merely move in and occupy the unused space of the human brain. I sow the seeds of negative thought in the minds of people so I can occupy and control the space!

Q You must have many tricks and devices by which you gain and hold control of the human mind.

A. To be sure, I employ tricks and devices to control human thought. My devices are clever ones too.

Q Go ahead and describe your clever tricks, Your Majesty.

A. One of my cleverest devices for mind control is fear. I plant the seed of fear in the minds of people, and as these seeds germinate and grow, through use, I control the space they occupy. The six most effective fears are the fear of poverty, criticism, ill health, loss of love, old age, and death.

Q Which of these six fears serves you most often, Your Majesty?

A. The first and the last—poverty and death! At one time or another during life I tighten my grip on all people through one or both of these. I plant these fears in the minds of people so deftly that they believe them to be their own creation. I accomplish this end by making people believe I am standing just beyond the entrance gate of the next life, waiting to claim them after death for eternal punishment. Of course I cannot punish anyone, except in that person's own mind, through some form of fear—but fear of the thing which does not exist is just as useful to me as fear of that which does exist. All forms of fear extend the space I occupy in the human mind.

Q Your Majesty, will you explain how you gained this control over human beings?

A. The story is too long to be told in a few words. It began over a million years ago, when the first man began to think. Up to that time I had control over all mankind, but enemies of mine discovered the power of positive thought, placed it in the minds of men, and then began a battle on my part to remain in control. So far, I have done quite well by myself, having lost only 2 percent of the people to the opposition.

Q I take it from your answer that men who think are your enemies. Is that right?
A. It is not right, but it is correct.

Q Tell me something more about the world in which you live.
A. I live wherever I choose. Time and space do not exist for me. I am a force best described to you as energy. My favorite physical dwelling place, as I have told you, is the minds of the earthbound. I control a part of the brain space of every human being. The amount of space I occupy in each individual's mind depends upon how little and what sort of thinking that person does. As I have told you, I cannot entirely control any person who thinks.

Q You speak of your opposition. What do you mean by that?
A. My opponent controls all the positive forces of the world, such as love, faith, hope, and optimism. My opponent also controls the positive factors of all natural law throughout the universe, the forces which keep the earth and the planets and all the stars balanced in their courses, but these forces are meek in comparison with those which operate in the human mind under my control. You see, I do not seek to control stars and planets. I prefer the control of human minds.

Q Where did you acquire your power, and by what means do you add to it?
A. I add to my power by appropriating the mind-power of the earthbound, as they come through the gate at the time of death. Ninety-eight out of every 100 who come back to my plane from the earth plane are taken over by me and their mind-power is added to my being. I get all who come over with any form of fear. You see I am constantly at work, preparing the minds of people before death, so I can appropriate them when they come back to my plane.

Q: Will you tell me how you go about your job of preparing human minds so you can control them?

A. I have countless ways of gaining control of human minds while they are still on the earth plane. My greatest weapon is poverty. I deliberately discourage people from accumulating material wealth because poverty discourages men from thinking and makes them easy prey for me. My next best friend is ill health. An unhealthy body discourages thinking. Then I have countless thousands of workers on earth who aid me in gaining control of human minds. I have these agents placed in every calling. They represent every race and creed, every religion.

Q: Who are your greatest enemies on earth, Your Majesty?

A. All who inspire people to think and act on their own initiative are my enemies. Such men as Socrates, Confucius, Voltaire, Emerson, Thomas Paine, and Abraham Lincoln. And you are not doing me any good either.

Q: Is it true that you use men who have great wealth?

A. As I have already told you, poverty is always my friend because it discourages independence of thought and encourages fear in the minds of men. Some wealthy men serve my cause while others do me great damage, depending upon how the wealth is used. The great Rockefeller fortune, for example, is one of my worst enemies.

Q: That is interesting, Your Majesty; will you tell me why you fear the Rockefeller fortune more than others?

A. The Rockefeller money is being used to isolate and conquer diseases of the physical body, in all parts of the world. Disease has always been one of my most effective weapons. The fear of ill health is second only to the fear of poverty. The Rockefeller money is uncovering new secrets of nature in a hundred different directions, all of which are designed to help men take and keep possession of their own minds. It is encouraging new and better methods of feeding, clothing, and housing people. It is wiping out the slums in the large cities, the places where my favorite allies are found It is financing campaigns for better government and helping to wipe out dishonesty in politics. It is helping to set higher standards in business practice and encouraging businessmen to conduct business by the Golden Rule; and that is not doing my cause any good.

Q What about these boys and girls who are said to be on the road to hell? Are you in control of them?

A. Well, I can answer that question only with "yes and no." I have corrupted the minds of the young by teaching them to drink and smoke, but they have me baffled through their tendency to think for themselves.

Q You say you have corrupted the minds of the young people with liquor and cigarettes. I can understand how liquor might destroy the power of independent thought but do not see what cigarettes have to do with helping your cause.

A. You may not know it, but cigarettes break down the power of persistence; they destroy the power of endurance; they destroy the ability to concentrate; they deaden and undermine the imaginative faculty, and help in other ways to keep people from using their minds most effectively.

Do you know I have millions of people, young and old, of both sexes, who smoke two packages of cigarettes a day? That means I have millions of people who are gradually destroying their power of resistance. One day I shall add to their habit of cigarette smoking other thought-destroying habits, until I shall have gained control of their minds.

Habits come in pairs, triplets, and quadruplets. Any habit which weakens one's will power invites a flock of its relatives to move in and take possession of the mind. The cigarette habit not only lowers the power of resistance and discourages persistence, but it invites looseness in other human relationships.

Q I never thought that cigarettes were a tool of destruction, Your Majesty, but your explanation throws a different light on the subject. How many converts to the habit do you now claim?

A. I am proud of my record. Millions are now victims, and the number is increasing daily. Soon I shall have most of the world indulging in the habit. In thousands of families I now have followers of the habit, including every member of the family. Very young boys and girls are beginning to take up the habit. They are learning how to smoke by observing their parents and older brothers and sisters.

Q Which do you consider to be your greater tool for gaining control of human minds—cigarettes or liquor?

A. Without hesitation I would say cigarettes. Once I get a young person to join my two-package-a-day club, I have no trouble in inducing that person to take on the habit of liquor, over-indulgence of sex, and all other related habits which destroy independence of thought and action.

Q Your Majesty, when I began this interview I had you all wrong. I thought you were a fraud and a fake, but I see now that you are quite real and very powerful.

A. Your apology is accepted, but you need not have bothered. Millions of people have questioned my power, and I got most of them at the gate as they came over.

I ask no person to believe in me. I prefer that people fear me. I am no beggar! I take what I want by cleverness and force. Begging people to believe is the business of my opposition—not mine.

Q Your Majesty will please pardon my rudeness, but I would not be able to look myself in the face again if I did not tell you, here and now, that you are the damnedest fiend ever to be turned loose on innocent people.

I always had the wrong conception of you. I thought you were kind enough to let people alone while they were living, that you merely tortured their souls after death. Now I learn, from your own brazen confession, that you destroy their right to freedom of thought and cause them to go through a living hell on earth. What do you have to say to that?

A. I get what I want by exercising self-control. It is not so good for my own business, but I suggest you emulate me instead of criticizing me. You call yourself a thinker, and you are. Otherwise you would never have forced this interview on me. But you will never be the sort of thinker that frightens me unless you gain and exercise greater control over your own emotions.

Q. Let us get away from personalities. I came here to learn more about you, not to discuss myself. Please go ahead and tell me of the many tricks you have devised for gaining control of the human mind. What is your most powerful weapon just now?

A. That is a difficult question to answer. I have so many devices for entering human minds and controlling them that it is difficult to say which are the most powerful. Right at the moment I am trying to bring about another world war. My friends here in Washington are helping me to involve America in the war. If I can start the world to killing on a wholesale basis, I shall be able to put into operation my favorite device for mind control. It is what you may call mass fear. I used this device to bring about the other World War in 1914. I used it to bring about the economic depression in 1929, and if my opposition had not double-crossed me, I would now be in possession of every man, woman, and child in the world. You can see for yourself how near I came to world domination—the thing I have been struggling to attain for thousands of years.

Q. Yes, I see your point. Who wouldn't? You are a very ingenious manipulator of the minds of people. Is your devilish business carried on only through people of high position and great influence?

A. Oh, no! I use the minds of people in all walks of life. As a matter of fact, I prefer the type of person who makes no pretense of thinking; I can manipulate that sort of person without difficulty. I could not control 98 percent of the people of the world if all people were skilled in thinking for themselves.

Q. I am interested in the welfare of those people whom you claim to control. Therefore, I wish you to tell me all of the tricks by which you enter and control their minds. I want a complete confession from you, so begin with your cleverest trick.

A. This is suicide you are forcing on me, but I am helpless! So settle down and I will place in your hands the weapon by which millions of your fellow-earthbound will defend themselves against me.

STUDY GUIDE

Chapter 3:
A Strange Interview with the Devil

1. Napoleon Hill opens this chapter by sharing the story of his unfortunate demise during the Depression in 1929. He saw the Great Depression as an opportunity to learn whether his philosophy of self-determination was practical or a mere theory. Write about a situation that tested you in your life. In retrospect, do you believe it supported or countered your belief system at that time? Please explain.
2. Did the adversity you experienced "bring a seed of equivalent advantage"? Please explain.
3. Have you ever found yourself "paralyzed with indecision"? Describe the situation and what you believe pulled you into that state.
4. Napoleon Hill attributes a great deal of the challenges he faced to working as a "lone wolf" as opposed to joining in a Master Mind (two or more minds working to a definite end). Have you ever found yourself stuck in an attempt to work through something alone, as opposed to working with others? If so, did you eventually reach out to others? Please explain.

An Analysis
5. Napoleon Hill shares that it is not important whether he conducted an interview with an actual or imagined Devil. What is most important is the contents of the exchange. Do you believe in a being that is a Devil or more of an energetic negativity that one can be consumed by? Please explain.
6. The Devil is referred to as "Mr. Earthbound." Why do you think he was referenced as such.

Here Begins the Interview with the Devil
7. Napoleon Hill stated that he "uncovered a secret code" by which he could pick up the Devil's thoughts. Do you believe this to be true? Why or why not?

8. The Devil claimed to have control over 98 percent of the world's people. Do you believe that this could be the case now in the world? Why or why not? Please explain.

9. The Devil stated, "I live in the minds of people who fear me." Do you fear the Devil? How might that fear energize such negativity? Please explain.

10. The Devil goes on to explain that he is the negative part of the atom—that life would not exist without him. Do you believe this to be true? Why or why not?

11. The Devil stated he is not a "beast with a forked tongue and a spiked tail" but that he is a force that is a necessary part of all of life. Do you believe this to be true? Why or why not?

12. The Devil claimed to control negative thoughts, and his opposition controls the positive ones. Do you believe this could be possible? Why or why not?

13. The Devil shares that one of his most potent and clever tricks for controlling minds is planting the seed of fear in them. He goes on to share that the six most effective fears are the fear of poverty, criticism, ill health, loss of love, old age, and death. Which of these fears most occupies your mind at this time?

14. The fear of poverty and the fear of death are the two that most serve the Devil. On a scale from 1 to 10 (1 being "not at all" and 10 being "very much so"), rate how fearful you are of poverty. Then on a scale from 1 to 10, rate how fearful you are of death.

    1 —— 2 —— 3 —— 4 —— 5 —— 6 —— 7 —— 8 —— 9 —— 10
    1 —— 2 —— 3 —— 4 —— 5 —— 6 —— 7 —— 8 —— 9 —— 10

15. The Devil states that he doesn't wait to claim us after death for eternal punishment. The punishment rests within fearful minds. Do you feel tormented by your fears? Please explain.

16. Napoleon Hill discovered that men who think are the enemies of the Devil—that he cannot control the mind of those who think. Do you believe yourself to be a "thinking" man or woman? Please explain.

17. The Devil claimed to gain control of man through poverty. He deliberately discourages people from accumulating material wealth. Do you struggle with a lack of consciousness? Write about the current relationship you have with poverty and financial abundance.

18. What percentage of control do you believe lack-consciousness occupies in your brain?

19. The Devil also shares that an unhealthy body discourages thinking. Write a list of the health challenges you are currently facing.

20. What percentage of your thoughts do you believe are occupied by ill health?

21. The Devil shares that his greatest enemies on earth are "all who inspire people to think and act on their own initiative." Contemplate your life and make a list of those whom you have inspired and how you did so, knowing that doing so has thwarted negativity.

22. The Devil lists Socrates, Confucius, Voltaire, Emerson, Thomas Paine, and Abraham Lincoln as men who are powerful because they think and act of their own initiatives. Research and list as least one woman who has done the same. Write about your findings.

23. The Devil sites Rockefeller as one of his greatest enemies because of the myriad ways in which he does good on the earth with his money. Contemplate the ways in which you have done good in the world with your money. Be sure to focus on all ways—they don't have to be big; every effort counts.

24. The Devil lists the use of alcohol and cigarette smoking as means by which he can weaken the minds of the young. He states that these habits destroy the power of persistence, endurance, concentration, and imagination. List other vises that you believe currently have this effect on humankind such as cell phone over-usage, video games, and vaping.

25. Are there any vices that you have which you believe are affecting your thinking and decision-making capacities? If so, list them.

26. Judging yourself for having these vices may only serve to create self-shame and only add to your demise. Can you take a moment and give yourself some compassion and appreciation for admitting to having them, and honoring that you have the courage to own them? Take at least five minutes to do so. Then write about any thoughts, feelings, or insights you gained doing so.

27. The Devil asserts that habits come in pairs, triplets, and quadruplets. Make a list of other habits you have that you believe to be self-destructive.

28. Napoleon Hill shares that he never considered the Devil as an entity that does not merely torture souls after death, but also does so while they are living. Have you considered this—that this existence is a living hell for many now? Please describe your thoughts and feelings.

29. The Devil cites mass fear that is caused by something like a world war as a great means of instilling fear in great numbers of humans. Make a list of how the Devil is currently manipulating masses of humans in the world today.

Chapter 4

Drifting with the Devil

Q Tell me first about your most clever trick—the one you use to ensnare the greatest number of people.
   A. If you force me to give away this secret, it will mean my loss of millions of people now living and still greater numbers of millions as yet unborn. I beg of you, permit me to pass this one question unanswered.

Q So His Majesty the Devil fears a mere humble earthbound creature! Is that right?
   A. It is not right, but it is true. You have no right to rob me of my most necessary tool of trade. For millions of years I have dominated earthbound creatures through fear and ignorance. Now you come along and would destroy my use of these weapons by forcing me to tell how I use them. Do you not realize that you will break my grip on every person who heeds this confession you are forcing from me? Have you no mercy? Have you no sense of humor?
   Have you no sportsmanship?

Q Stop stalling, and start confessing. Who are you to ask mercy of one whom you would destroy if you could? Who are you to talk of sportsmanship and a sense of humor? You, who by your own confession have set up a living hell on earth, where you punish innocent people through their fears and ignorance. As for minding my own business, that is just what I am doing when I force you to tell how you control people through their own minds. My business, if it can be called a business, is helping to unlock the doors of the self-made prisons in which men and women are confined because of the fears you have planted in their minds.

A. My greatest weapon over human beings consists of two secret principles by which I gain control of their minds. I will speak first of the principle of habit, through which I silently enter the minds of people. By operating through this principle, I establish (I wish I could avoid using this word) the habit of drifting. When a person begins to drift on any subject, he is headed straight toward the gates of what you earthbound call hell.

Q Describe all the ways in which you induce people to drift. Define the word and tell us exactly what you mean by it.

A. I can best define the word "drift" by saying that people who think for themselves never drift, while those who do little or no thinking for themselves are drifters. A drifter is one who permits himself to be influenced and controlled by circumstances outside of his own mind. He would rather let me occupy his mind and do his thinking than go to the trouble of thinking for himself. A drifter is one who accepts whatever life throws in his way without making a protest or putting up a fight. He doesn't know what he wants from life and spends all of his time getting just that. A drifter has lots of opinions, but they are not his own. Most of them are supplied by me.

A drifter is one who is too lazy mentally to use his own brain. That is the reason I can take control of people's thinking and plant my own ideas in their minds.

Q I think I understand what a drifter is. Tell me the exact habits of people by which you induce them to drift through life. Start by telling me when and how you first gain control of a person's mind.

A. My control over the mind of a human being is obtained while the person is young. Sometimes I lay the foundation for my control of a mind before the owner of it is born, by manipulating the minds of that person's parents. Sometimes I go further back than this and prepare people for my control through what you earthbound call "physical heredity." You see, therefore, I have two approaches to the mind of a person.

Q Yes. Go on and describe these two doors by which you enter and control the minds of human beings.

A. As I have stated, I help to bring people into your world with weak brains by giving to them, before birth, as many as possible of the weaknesses of their ancestors. You call this principle "physical heredity." After people are born I make use of what you earthbound call "environment" as a means of controlling them. This is where the principle of habit enters. The mind is nothing more than the sum total of one's habits! One by one I enter the mind and establish habits, which lead finally to my absolute domination of the mind.

Q Tell me of the most common habits by which you control the minds of people.

A. That is one of my cleverest tricks: I enter the minds of people through thoughts which they believe to be their own. Those most useful to me are fear, superstition, avarice, greed, lust, revenge, anger, vanity, and plain laziness. Through one or more of these I can enter any mind, at any age, but I get my best results when I take charge of a mind while it is young, before its owner has learned how to close any of these nine doors. Then I can set up habits which keep the doors ajar forever.

Q I am catching on to your methods. Now let us go back to the habit of drifting. Tell us all about that habit since you say it is your cleverest trick in controlling the minds of people.

A. As I said before, I start people drifting during their youth. I induce them to drift through school without knowing what occupation they wish to follow in life. Here I catch the majority of people. Habits are related. Drift in one direction and soon you will be drifting in all directions. I also use environmental habits to give me a definite grip on my victims.

Q I see. You make it your business to train children in the habit of drifting by inducing them to go through school without aim or purpose. Now tell me of some of your other tricks with which you cause people to become drifters.

A. Well, my second best trick in developing the habit of drifting is one that I put into operation with the aid of parents and public schoolteachers and religious instructors.

I warn you not to force me to mention this trick. Do not disclose this trick. If you do so, you will be hated by my co-workers who help me use this trick. If you publish this confession in book form, your book will be barred from the public schools. It will be blacklisted by most of the religious leaders. It will be hidden from children by many parents. The newspapers will not dare to give reviews of your book. Millions of people will hate you for writing the book.

In fact, no one will like you or your book except those who think, and you know how very few there are of this sort! My advice to you is to let me skip the description of my second best trick.

Q So for my own good you wish to withhold the description of your second best trick. No one will like my book except those who think, eh? Very well, go ahead and answer.

A. You'll regret this, Mr. Earthbound, but the joke is on you. By this mistake of yours you will divert attention from me to yourself.

My co-workers, of whom there are millions, will forget about me and hate you for uncovering my methods.

Q. Never mind about me. Tell me all about this second best trick of yours with which you induce people to drift with you to hell.

A. My second best trick is not second at all. It is first! It is first because without it I never could gain control of the minds of the youths. Parents, schoolteachers, religious instructors, and many other adults unknowingly serve my purpose by helping me to destroy in children the habit of thinking for themselves. They go about their work in various ways, never suspecting what they are doing to the minds of children or the real cause of the children's mistakes.

Q. I can hardly believe you, Your Majesty. I have always believed that children's best friends were those closest to them, their parents, their schoolteachers, and their religious instructors. Where would children go for dependable guidance if not to those who have charge of them?

A. That is where my cleverness comes in. There is the exact explanation of how I control 98 percent of the people of the world. I take possession of people during their youth, before they come into possession of their own minds, by using those who are in charge of them. I especially need the help of those who give children their religious instruction, because it is here that I break down independent thought and start people on the habit of drifting, by confusing their minds with unprovable ideas concerning a world of which they know nothing. It is here also that I plant in the minds of children the greatest of all fears—the fear of hell!

Q. I understand that it is easy for you to frighten children with threats of hell, but how do you continue to make them fear you and your hell after they grow up and learn to think for themselves?

A. Children grow up, but they do not always learn to think for themselves! Once I capture the mind of a child, through fear,

I weaken that child's ability to reason and to think for himself, and that weakness goes with the child all through life.

Q Is that not taking unfair advantage of a human being by contaminating his mind before he comes into full possession of it?

A. Everything is fair that I can use to further my ends. I have no foolish limitations of right and wrong. Might is right with me. I use every known human weakness to gain and keep control of the human mind.

Q I understand your devilish nature! Now let us get back to further discussion of your methods of inducing people to drift to hell here on earth. From your confession I see that you take charge of children while their minds are young and pliable. Tell me more of how you use parents, teachers, and religious leaders to ensnare people into drifting.

A. One of my favorite tricks is to coordinate the efforts of parents and religious instructors so they work together in helping me to destroy the children's power to think for themselves. I use many religious instructors to undermine the courage and power of independent thought of children, by teaching them to fear me; but I use parents to aid the religious leaders in this great work of mine.

Q How do parents help religious leaders destroy their children's power to think for themselves? I never heard of such a monstrosity!

A. I accomplish this through a very clever trick. I cause the parents to teach their children to believe as the parents do in connection with religion, politics, marriage, and other important subjects. In this way, as you can see, when I gain control of the mind of a person I can easily perpetuate the control by causing that person to help me fasten it upon the minds of his offspring.

Q In what other ways do you use parents to convert children into drifters?

A. I cause children to become drifters by following the example of their parents, most of whom I have already taken over and bound eternally to my cause. In some parts of the world I gain mastery over children's minds and subdue their will power in exactly the same way that men break and subdue animals of lower intelligence. It makes no difference to me how a child's will is subdued, as long as it fears something. I will enter its mind through that fear and limit the child's power to think independently.

Q It seems that you go out of your way to keep people from thinking.

A. Yes. Accurate thought is death to me. I cannot exist in the minds of those who think accurately. I do not mind people thinking as long as they think in terms of fear, discouragement, hopelessness, and destructiveness. When they begin to think in constructive terms of faith, courage, hope, and definiteness of purpose, they immediately become allies of my opposition and are therefore lost to me.

Q I am beginning to understand how you gain control of the minds of children through the help of their parents and religious instructors, but I do not see how the schoolteachers help you in this damnable work.

A. Schoolteachers help me gain control of the minds of children not so much by what they teach the children as because of what they do not teach them. The entire public school system is so administered that it helps my cause by teaching children almost everything except how to use their own minds and think independently. I live in fear that someday some courageous person will reverse the present system of school teaching and deal my cause a death blow by allowing the students to become the instructors, using those who now serve as teachers only as guides to help the children establish ways and means of developing their own minds from within. When that time comes, the schoolteachers will no longer belong to my staff.

Q. I was under the impression that the purpose of all schooling was to help children to think.

A. That may be the purpose of schooling, but the system in most of the schools of the world does not carry out the purpose. School children are taught not to develop and use their own minds, but to adopt and use the thoughts of others. This sort of schooling destroys the capacity for independent thought, except in a few rare cases where children rely so definitely upon their own will power that they refuse to allow others to do their thinking. Accurate thought is the business of my opposition, not mine!

Q. What relationship, if any, has your opposition with the homes, the churches, and the schools? Your reply to this question should be interesting.

A. Here is where I make use of some more of my clever tricks. I cause it to appear that everything done by the parents, the schoolteachers, and the religious instructors is being done by my opposition.

This diverts attention from me while I manipulate the minds of the young. When religious instructors try to teach children the virtues of my opposition, they generally do so by frightening them with my name. That is all I ask of them. I kindle the flame of fear into proportions which destroy the child's power to think accurately. In the public schools the teachers further my cause by keeping the children so busy cramming non-essential information into their minds they have no opportunity to think accurately or to analyze correctly the things their instructors teach them.

Q. Do you claim, for your cause, all those who are bound by the habit of drifting?

A. No. Drifting is only one of my tricks through which I take over the power of independent thought. Before a drifter becomes my permanent property, I must lead him on and ensnare him with another trick. I will tell you about this other trick after I finish describing my methods of converting people into drifters.

Q Do you mean you have a method by which you can cause people to drift so far away from self-determination that they can never save themselves?
A. Yes, a definite method: And it is so effective it never fails.

Q Do I understand you to claim your method is so powerful your opposition cannot reclaim those whom you have permanently ensnared through drifting?
A. I claim just that! Do you think I would control so many people if my opposition could prevent me? Nothing can stop me from controlling people except people themselves.

Nothing can stop me except the power of accurate thought. People who think accurately do not drift on any subject. They recognize the power of their own minds. Moreover, they take over that power and yield it to no person or influence.

Q Go ahead and tell me more of the methods by which you cause people to drift to hell with you!
A. I cause people to drift on every subject through which I can control independent thought and action. Take the subject of health, for example. I cause most people to eat too much food and the wrong sort of food. This leads to indigestion and destroys the power of accurate thought. If the public schools and the churches taught children more about proper eating, they would do my cause irreparable damage.

Marriage: I cause men and women to drift into marriage without plan or purpose designed to convert the relationship into harmony. Here is one of my most effective methods of converting people into the habit of drifting. I cause married people to bicker and nag one another over money matters. I cause them to quarrel over the bringing up of their children. I engage them in unpleasant controversies over their intimate relationships and in disagreements over friends and social activities. I keep them so busy finding fault with one another that they never have time to do anything else long enough to break the habit of drifting.

Occupation: I teach people to become drifters by causing them to drift out of school into the first job they can find, with no definite aim or purpose except to make a living. Through this trick I keep millions of people in fear of poverty all their lives. Through this fear I lead them slowly but surely onward until they reach the point beyond which no individual ever has broken the drifting habit.

Savings: I cause people to spend freely and to save sparingly or not at all, until I take complete control of them through their fear of poverty.

Environment: I cause people to drift into inharmonious and unpleasant environments in the home, in their places of occupation, in their relationship with relatives and acquaintances, and to remain there until I claim them through the habit of drifting.

Dominating Thoughts: I cause people to drift into the habit of thinking negative thoughts. This leads to negative acts and involves people in controversies and fills their minds with fears, thus paving the way for me to enter and control their minds. When I move in, I do so by appealing to people through negative thoughts which they believe to be their own. I plant the seeds of negative thought in the minds of people through the pulpit, the newspapers, the moving pictures, the radio, and all other popular methods of appeal to the mind. I cause people to allow me to do their thinking for them because they are too lazy and too indifferent to think for themselves.

Q I conclude from what you say that drifting and procrastination are the same. Is that true?

A. Yes, that is correct. Any habit which causes one to procrastinate—to put off reaching a definite decision—leads to the habit of drifting.

Q Is man the only creature who drifts?

A. Yes. All other creatures move in response to definite laws of nature.

Man alone defies nature's laws and drifts when he wills.

Everything outside the minds of men is controlled by my opposition, by laws so definite that drifting is impossible. I control the minds of men solely because of their habit of drifting, which is only another way of saying that I control the minds of men only because they neglect or refuse to control and use their own minds.

Q This is getting to be pretty deep stuff for a mere human being. Let us get back to the discussion of something less abstract. Please tell me how this drifting habit affects people in the everyday walks of life and tell me in terms the average person can understand.

A. I would prefer to keep this interview up among the stars!

Q No doubt you would. That would save you from being exposed. But let us come back to earth. Tell me now what drifting is doing to us as a nation here in the United States.

A. Frankly, I may as well tell you that I hate the United States as only the Devil can hate.

Q That is interesting. What is the cause of this hatred?

A. The cause was born on July 4, 1776, when fifty-six men signed a document which destroyed my chances of controlling the nation. You know that document as the Declaration of Independence. Had it not been for the influence of that damnable document, I would now have a dictator running the country and I would stop this right to free speech and independent thought that is threatening my rule on earth.

Q**Am I to understand from what you say that nations controlled by self-appointed dictators belong in your camp?**
A. There are no self-appointed dictators. I appoint them all. Moreover, I manipulate them and direct them in their work. Nations run by my dictators know what they want and take it by force. Look what I have done through Mussolini in Italy! Look what I am doing through Hitler in Germany. Look what I am doing through Stalin in Russia. My dictators run those nations for me because the people have been subdued through the habit of drifting. My dictators do no drifting. That is why they rule for me the millions of people under their control.

Q**What would happen if Mussolini, Stalin, and Hitler turned traitors and disavowed you and your rule?**
A. That will not happen because I have them too well bribed. I am paying each of them with the sop of his own vanity, by making him believe he is acting on his own account. That is another trick of mine.

Q**Let us come back to the United States and learn something of what you are doing to convert people into the habit of drifting.**
A. Right now I am paving the way for a dictatorship by sowing the seeds of fear and uncertainty in the minds of the people.

Q**Through whom are you carrying on your work?**
A. Mainly through the President. I am destroying his influence with the people by causing him to drift on the question of a working agreement between employers and their employees. If I can induce him to drift for another year, he will be so thoroughly discredited I can hand over the country to a dictator. If the President continues to drift, I will paralyze personal freedom in the United States just as I destroyed it in Spain, Italy, Germany, and England.

Q What you say leads me to the conclusion that drifting is a weakness which inevitably ends in failure, whether among individuals or nations. Is that your claim?

A. Drifting is the most common cause of failure in every walk of life. I can control anyone whom I can induce to form the habit of drifting on any subject. The reason for this is twofold. First, the drifter is just so much putty in my hands, to be molded into whatever pattern I choose, because drifting destroys the power of individual initiative. Second, the drifter cannot get help from my opposition, because the opposition is not attracted to anything so soft and useless.

Q Is that why a few people are wealthy while the majority of people are poor?

A. That is exactly the reason. Poverty, like physical illness, is a contagious disease. You find it always among the drifters, never among those who know what they want and are determined to get just that! It may mean something to you when I call your attention to the fact that the non-drifters, whom I do not control, and those who possess most of the wealth of the world, happen to be the same people.

Q I have always understood that money was the root of all evil, that the poor and the meek would inherit heaven, while the wealthy would pass into your hands. What have you to say of that claim?

A. Men who know how to get the material things of life generally know how to keep out of the hands of the Devil as well. The ability to acquire things is contagious. Drifters acquire nothing except that which no one else wants. If more people had definite aims and stronger desires for material and spiritual riches, I would have fewer victims.

Q. I assume, from what you say, that you do not claim fellowship with the industrial leaders. Evidently they are not friends of yours.

A. Friends of mine? I'll tell you what sort of friends of mine they are. They have belted the entire country with good roads, thus bringing into close communion the people of both city and country. They have converted ores into steel, with which they have built the skeletons of great skyscrapers. They have harnessed electrical power and converted it into a thousand uses, all designed to give man time to think. They have provided through the automobile personal transportation to the humblest citizen, thus giving to everyone the freedom of travel. They have provided every home with instantaneous news of what is happening in all parts of the world through the aid of the radio.

They have reared libraries in every city, town, and hamlet and have filled them with books giving to all who read a complete outline of the most useful knowledge mankind has gathered from his experiences. They have given the humblest citizen the right to express his own opinion on any subject, anytime, anywhere, without fear of molestation, and they have seen to it that every citizen may help make his own laws, levy his own taxes, and manage his own country through the ballot. These are but some of the things the industrial leaders have done to give every citizen the privilege of becoming a non-drifter. Do you think these men have helped my cause?

Q. Who are some of the present-day non-drifters over whom you have no control?

A. I have control over no non-drifter, present or past. I control the weak, not those who think for themselves.

Q. Go ahead and describe a typical drifter. Give your description point by point so I can recognize a drifter when I see him.

A. The first thing you will notice about a drifter is his total lack of a major purpose in life.

He will be conspicuous by his lack of self-confidence.

He will never accomplish anything requiring thought and effort. He spends all he earns and more too, if he can get credit.

He will be sick or ailing from some real or imaginary cause, and calling to high heaven if he suffers the least physical pain.

He will have little or no imagination.

He will lack enthusiasm and initiative to begin anything he is not forced to undertake, and he will plainly express his weakness by taking the line of least resistance whenever he can do so.

He will be ill-tempered and lacking in control over his emotions.

His personality will be without magnetism and it will not attract other people.

He will have opinions on everything but accurate knowledge of nothing. He may be jack-of-all trades but good at none.

He will neglect to cooperate with those around him, even those on whom he must depend for food and shelter.

He will make the same mistake over and over again, never profiting by failure.

He will be narrow-minded and intolerant on all subjects, ready to crucify those who may disagree with him.

He will expect everything of others but be willing to give little or nothing in return.

He may begin many things but he will complete nothing.

He will be loud in his condemnation of his government, but he will never tell you definitely how it can be improved.

He will never reach decisions on anything if he can avoid it, and if he is forced to decide he will reverse himself at the first opportunity.

He will eat too much and exercise too little.

He will take a drink of liquor if someone else will pay for it. He will gamble if he can do it "on the cuff."

He will criticize others who are succeeding in their chosen calling.

In brief, the drifter will work harder to get out of thinking than most others work in earning a good living.

He will tell a lie rather than admit his ignorance on any subject.

If he works for others, he will criticize them to their backs and flatter them to their faces.

Q. You have given me a graphic description of the drifter. Please now describe the non-drifter so that I may recognize him on sight.

A. The first sign of a non-drifter is this: He is always engaged in doing something definite, through some well-organized plan which is definite. He has a major goal in life toward which he is always working, and many minor goals, all of which lead toward his central scheme.

The tone of his voice, the quickness of his step, the sparkle in his eyes, the quickness of his decisions clearly mark him as a person who knows exactly what he wants and is determined to get it, no matter how long it may take or what price he must pay.

If you ask him questions, he gives you direct answers and never falls back on evasions or resorts to subterfuge.

He extends many favors to others, but accepts favors sparingly or not at all.

He will be found up front whether he is playing a game or fighting a war. If he does not know the answers he will say so frankly.

He has a good memory; never offers an alibi for his shortcomings.

He never blames others for his mistakes no matter if they deserve the blame.

He used to be known as a go-getter, but in modern times he is called a go-giver. You will find him running the biggest business in town, living on the best street, driving the best automobile, and making his presence felt wherever he happens to be.

He is an inspiration to all who come into contact with his mind.

The major distinguishing feature of the non-drifter is this: He has a mind of his own and uses it for all purposes.

Q Is the non-drifter born with some mental, physical, or spiritual advantage not available to the drifter?

A. No. The major difference between the drifter and the non-drifter is something equally available to both. It is simply the prerogative right of each to use his own mind and think for himself.

Q What brief message would you send to the typical drifter if you wished to cure him of this evil habit?

A. I would admonish him to wake up and give!

Q Give what?

A. Some form of service useful to as many people as possible.

Q So the non-drifter is supposed to give, is he?

A. Yes, if he expects to get! And he must give before he gets!

Q Some people doubt that you exist.

A. I wouldn't worry about that if I were you. Those who are ready to be converted from the habit of drifting will recognize the authenticity of this interview by its soundness of counsel. The others are not worth the trouble it would take to convert them.

Q Why do you not try to stop me from publishing this confession I am wringing from you?

A. Because that would be the surest of all ways to guarantee you will publish it. I have a better plan than trying to suppress publication of my confession. I will urge you to go ahead with the publication, then sit back and watch you suffer when some of my faithful drifters begin to make things hot for you. I will not need to deny your story. My followers will do that for me—see if they don't.

STUDY GUIDE

Chapter 4:
Drifting with the Devil

1. Napoleon Hill challenges the Devil to share his most clever trick. The Devil eventually shares that the first involves the principle of habit. He goes on to share that through the habit of "drifting," humans will experience earthbound hell. He defines a drifter as "one who permits himself to be influenced and controlled by circumstances outside of his own mind." Reflect on your current situation. What outer influences do you believe have some control of your mind? List them.

2. Drifters are further defined as individuals who do not think for themselves—people who accept what comes their way without protest or putting up a fight. What have you fought for in your life? Make a list.

3. Drifters don't know what they want in their lives. Are you clear on what you want in your life?

4. The two means by which the Devil controls minds are (1) by manipulating the minds of the parents before children are born and (2) through physical heredity. Do you believe this to be true? Why or why not?

5. The Devil defines the mind as "nothing more than the sum total of one's habits." Do you believe this to be true? Why or why not? Give an example in your life.

6. The Devil proceeds to share that he enters minds through thoughts that people believe to be their own. Have you ever considered that the thoughts you think may not be your own are part of a thought sphere (like the air you breathe is part of the atmosphere)? Take a moment to consider this. If you are NOT your thoughts, but a vessel through which they move, then how would your self-identity change? Take some time to consider this and write about any insights that arise.

7. The Devil makes use of fear, superstition, avarice, greed, lust, revenge, anger, vanity, and laziness as means by which he takes over people's minds. Do a personal inventory and on a scale from 1 to 10, rate the

degree to which you believe yourself to be trapped in the following habits (1 being "very little" and 10 being "very much so"):

Fear
1 — 2 — 3 — 4 — 5 — 6 — 7 — 8 — 9 — 10

Superstition
1 — 2 — 3 — 4 — 5 — 6 — 7 — 8 — 9 — 10

Avarice
1 — 2 — 3 — 4 — 5 — 6 — 7 — 8 — 9 — 10

Greed
1 — 2 — 3 — 4 — 5 — 6 — 7 — 8 — 9 — 10

Lust
1 — 2 — 3 — 4 — 5 — 6 — 7 — 8 — 9 — 10

Revenge
1 — 2 — 3 — 4 — 5 — 6 — 7 — 8 — 9 — 10

Anger
1 — 2 — 3 — 4 — 5 — 6 — 7 — 8 — 9 — 10

Vanity
1 — 2 — 3 — 4 — 5 — 6 — 7 — 8 — 9 — 10

Laziness
1 — 2 — 3 — 4 — 5 — 6 — 7 — 8 — 9 — 10

8. Controlling the youth by inducing them to go through school without any aim or purpose is a means by which the Devil controls minds. Do you believe our youth aimlessly drift through school more now than in Napoleon Hill's time. Why or why not? Please explain.

9. The Devil threatens that if Napoleon Hill shares his second secret in a book, he will be hated, scorned, and blacklisted by the masses. Napoleon charges on and demands an answer. The Devil shares that he uses the adults who most influence children to assist him with controlling them: their parents, their schoolteachers, and, most significantly, their religious instructors. Reflecting on your youth, how much influence did these adults have in your life?

10. Was the fear of hell taught to you? If so, by whom?

11. Does the fear of hell still affect your psyche? On a scale from 1 to 10, rate the degree to which you fear hell after death (1 being "very little" and 10 being "very much so"):
1 —— 2 —— 3 —— 4 —— 5 —— 6 —— 7 —— 8 —— 9 —— 10

12. The Devil asserts that he causes parents to teach their children to believe as the parents do in connection with religion, politics, marriage, and other subjects. Reflect on your childhood and write a list of your parents' beliefs in three areas. Then put a checkmark beside those beliefs that you follow and an X beside those from which you have broken away.

13. Do you believe that fear got in the way of your ability to independently think when you were a child? Write about a circumstance where fear of retribution or hell kept you from moving forward with something that was rooted in independence.

14. Were you able to break free of that fear or is there still residual remains of it in your psyche?

15. The Devil thrives on thoughts of fear, discouragement, hopelessness, and destructiveness. List the ways in which you believe you can be consumed by these four types of thoughts.

16. Constructive thinking in terms of faith, courage, hope, and definiteness of purpose are the Devil's enemies. List the ways in which you believe you are uplifted by these four types of thoughts.

17. What percentage of your thoughts do you believe are fear-based and, in comparison, what percentage you believe are courage-based?

18. The Devil says that he uses teachers as a means of discouraging independent thought and cultivating an ability to use their own minds. Do you think that the current school system within your culture has shifted into more independent thinking than was the norm during the 1930s? Please explain.

19. The Devil claims that when religious instructors try to teach children the virtues of his opposition, they do so by frightening them with his name. They "kindle the flame of fear" in a way that destroys children's power to think accurately. Have you ever experienced this in your life? Have you seen it played out in the lives of others? If so, how?

20. People who know their own minds and yield to no other person or influence cannot be affected by the Devil or negativity. In what ways do you currently find your mind influenced or swayed by external forces? List them.

21. Sometimes you may not be conscious of outer influences. They rest in the unawareness of your subconscious. Take a moment to quiet yourself and ask your subconscious self to awaken you to ways in which you are unconsciously influenced.

22. The Devil asserts that proper eating was not taught In school, and ultimately leads to indigestion and the destruction of the power of accurate thought. Nutrition is taught more at schools now. Do you believe that improper eating is still a problem that children face? Why or why not? What might be the cause?

23. On a scale from 1 to 10, rate the degree to which you practice healthy eating (1 being "very little" and 10 being "very much so"):

1 —— 2 —— 3 —— 4 —— 5 —— 6 —— 7 —— 8 —— 9 —— 10

24. The Devil further asserts that he makes couples drifters as they quarrel about money matters, raising their children, friends, and social activities. Regarding your familial relationships, on a scale from 1 to 10 (1 being "very little" and 10 being "very much so"), rate the degree to which you experience strife about the following:

Money Matters:

1 —— 2 —— 3 —— 4 —— 5 —— 6 —— 7 —— 8 —— 9 —— 10

Raising Children:

1 —— 2 —— 3 —— 4 —— 5 —— 6 —— 7 —— 8 —— 9 —— 10

Friendships:

1 —— 2 —— 3 —— 4 —— 5 —— 6 —— 7 —— 8 —— 9 —— 10

Social Activities:

1 —— 2 —— 3 —— 4 —— 5 —— 6 —— 7 —— 8 —— 9 —— 10

25. Regarding your occupation, are you fearfully remaining in a career that is not fulfilling? On a scale from 1 to 10 (1 being "very little" and 10 being "very much so"), rate the degree to which you are currently satisfied in your career:

1 —— 2 —— 3 —— 4 —— 5 —— 6 —— 7 —— 8 —— 9 —— 10

26. Regarding your savings, are you extreme in either saving or spending? On a scale from 1 to 10 (1 being "very little" and 10 being "very much so"), rate the degree to which you believe you have healthy savings:

1 —— 2 —— 3 —— 4 —— 5 —— 6 —— 7 —— 8 —— 9 —— 10

27. Regarding your environment, do you believe your home, work, and social environments to be balanced and healthy? On a scale from 1 to 10 (1 being "very little" and 10 being "very much so"), rate the degree to which you believe each to be healthy:

Home:

1 —— 2 —— 3 —— 4 —— 5 —— 6 —— 7 —— 8 —— 9 —— 10

Work:

1 —— 2 —— 3 —— 4 —— 5 —— 6 —— 7 —— 8 —— 9 —— 10

Social:

1 —— 2 —— 3 —— 4 —— 5 —— 6 —— 7 —— 8 —— 9 —— 10

28. Regarding your Dominating Thoughts. On a scale from 1 to 10 (1 being "very little" and 10 being "very much so"), rate the degree to which you believe your thoughts are primarily positive:

1 —— 2 —— 3 —— 4 —— 5 —— 6 —— 7 —— 8 —— 9 —— 10

29. Further regarding your Dominating Thoughts, seeds can be planted in your mind through the pulpit, newspapers, television, movies, radio, and social media. On a scale from 1 to 10 (1 being "very little" and 10 being "very much so"), rate the degree to which you believe yourself to be negatively influenced:

The Pulpit/Religious Messaging:

1 —— 2 —— 3 —— 4 —— 5 —— 6 —— 7 —— 8 —— 9 —— 10

Newspapers:

1 —— 2 —— 3 —— 4 —— 5 —— 6 —— 7 —— 8 —— 9 —— 10

Television:

1 —— 2 —— 3 —— 4 —— 5 —— 6 —— 7 —— 8 —— 9 —— 10

Movies:

1 —— 2 —— 3 —— 4 —— 5 —— 6 —— 7 —— 8 —— 9 —— 10

Radio:

1 —— 2 —— 3 —— 4 —— 5 —— 6 —— 7 —— 8 —— 9 —— 10

Social Media:

1 —— 2 —— 3 —— 4 —— 5 —— 6 —— 7 —— 8 —— 9 —— 10

30. Another term for drifting is procrastination. To what degree do you suffer from procrastination? On a scale from 1 to 10 (1 being "very little" and 10 being "very much so"), rate the degree to which you believe you suffer from procrastination:

1 —— 2 —— 3 —— 4 —— 5 —— 6 —— 7 —— 8 —— 9 —— 10

31. The Devil states that he hates the US because of the creation of the Declaration of Independence, and if it wasn't for that, our country could potentially be run by a dictator. Do you believe this issue to no longer be a threat to us? Please explain.

32. The Devil stated that he bribes dictators by making them believe that they are empowered by their own account. Reflect on your life. Have you personally credited yourself for all your achievements, or were you able to tap into humility, seeing the "other self" or source as the core to your achievements?

33. Keep in mind that this book was written before 1938, when Franklin D. Roosevelt was the president of the United States. The Devil stated that he was hoping to destroy the president's influence by inducing him to drift on the question of a working agreement between employers and their employees that will paralyze personal freedom. Do some research into the Roosevelt era of leadership. Do you think that Roosevelt was preoccupied with this issue to the point where it weakened him as a leader at that time? Please explain.

34. Roosevelt's initiatives to support American workers changed the trajectory of the workforce movement in the US. Looking back at the outcome his initiatives had since his leadership, do you believe that they worked for or against the progress and success of America as a country? In your opinion, did the Devil succeed?

35. Truman was Roosevelt's successor. Both presidents had a profound effect on the country at that time. While the world ended up in a war against Hitler, do you believe that Roosevelt and later Truman fell into a drifter stance and debilitated the country? Please explain.

36. The Devil likens poverty to a physical disease. Do you believe this to be so? Please explain.

37. The Devil claimed that if more people had "definite aims and stronger desires for material wealth and spiritual riches," he would have fewer victims. Do you believe this to be true? Please explain.

38. The Devil listed the ways in which industrial leaders supported the US and thwarted Roosevelt's negative initiatives. What current day leaders have supported the advancement of the American people in a positive way and how?

39. The Devil described the character traits of a drifter. Take some time to reflect honestly on your personality traits and the life you have carved out for yourself thus far. On a scale from 1 to 10 (1 being the lowest and 10 the highest), rate how much you display the following tendencies:

    Lack of Major Purpose in Life:
    1 — 2 — 3 — 4 — 5 — 6 — 7 — 8 — 9 — 10

    Lack of Self-Confidence:
    1 — 2 — 3 — 4 — 5 — 6 — 7 — 8 — 9 — 10

    No Savings/Poor Credit:
    1 — 2 — 3 — 4 — 5 — 6 — 7 — 8 — 9 — 10

    Physically Unhealthy:
    1 — 2 — 3 — 4 — 5 — 6 — 7 — 8 — 9 — 10

    Little to No Imagination:
    1 — 2 — 3 — 4 — 5 — 6 — 7 — 8 — 9 — 10

    Apathetic/Take the Line of Least Resistance:
    1 — 2 — 3 — 4 — 5 — 6 — 7 — 8 — 9 — 10

    Ill-Tempered/Unable to Control Emotions:
    1 — 2 — 3 — 4 — 5 — 6 — 7 — 8 — 9 — 10

    Lacking Charisma:
    1 — 2 — 3 — 4 — 5 — 6 — 7 — 8 — 9 — 10

    Many Opinions/Little Actual Knowledge:
    1 — 2 — 3 — 4 — 5 — 6 — 7 — 8 — 9 — 10

    Jack-of-All-Trades and a Master of None:
    1 — 2 — 3 — 4 — 5 — 6 — 7 — 8 — 9 — 10

Uncooperative:
1 — 2 — 3 — 4 — 5 — 6 — 7 — 8 — 9 — 10

Never Learns from Mistakes:
1 — 2 — 3 — 4 — 5 — 6 — 7 — 8 — 9 — 10

Narrow-Minded and Intolerant:
1 — 2 — 3 — 4 — 5 — 6 — 7 — 8 — 9 — 10

Selfish and Ungiving:
1 — 2 — 3 — 4 — 5 — 6 — 7 — 8 — 9 — 10

Does Not Complete Things:
1 — 2 — 3 — 4 — 5 — 6 — 7 — 8 — 9 — 10

Condemns the Government but Does Not Know How to Improve:
1 — 2 — 3 — 4 — 5 — 6 — 7 — 8 — 9 — 10

Indecisive:
1 — 2 — 3 — 4 — 5 — 6 — 7 — 8 — 9 — 10

Overeats and Does Little Exercise:
1 — 2 — 3 — 4 — 5 — 6 — 7 — 8 — 9 — 10

Drinks Too Much, Especially When Others Pay for It:
1 — 2 — 3 — 4 — 5 — 6 — 7 — 8 — 9 — 10

Gambles:
1 — 2 — 3 — 4 — 5 — 6 — 7 — 8 — 9 — 10

Criticizes the Success of Others:
1 — 2 — 3 — 4 — 5 — 6 — 7 — 8 — 9 — 10

Works Hard to Avoid Thinking:
1 — 2 — 3 — 4 — 5 — 6 — 7 — 8 — 9 — 10

Lies and Does Not Admit Wrongdoing:
1 — 2 — 3 — 4 — 5 — 6 — 7 — 8 — 9 — 10

Hypocrite and Two-Faced, Especially with Employers:
1 — 2 — 3 — 4 — 5 — 6 — 7 — 8 — 9 — 10

40. Tally your score in the twenty-four areas above. Your score is ___ /240.

41. The Devil then described the character traits of a nondrifter. As you did in the previous exercise, on a scale from 1 to 10 (1 being the lowest and 10 the highest), rate how much you display the following tendencies:

Definite:
1 — 2 — 3 — 4 — 5 — 6 — 7 — 8 — 9 — 10

Engaged:
1 — 2 — 3 — 4 — 5 — 6 — 7 — 8 — 9 — 10

Organized:
1 — 2 — 3 — 4 — 5 — 6 — 7 — 8 — 9 — 10

Have Major Life Goals:
1 — 2 — 3 — 4 — 5 — 6 — 7 — 8 — 9 — 10

Have Minor Life Goals:
1 — 2 — 3 — 4 — 5 — 6 — 7 — 8 — 9 — 10

Major and Minor Life Goals All Lead to Central Theme:
1 — 2 — 3 — 4 — 5 — 6 — 7 — 8 — 9 — 10

Direct in Communications:
1 — 2 — 3 — 4 — 5 — 6 — 7 — 8 — 9 — 10

Support Others and Very Self-Efficient:
1 — 2 — 3 — 4 — 5 — 6 — 7 — 8 — 9 — 10

Upfront and Honest When Playing Games or In War:
1 — 2 — 3 — 4 — 5 — 6 — 7 — 8 — 9 — 10

Honest and Upfront When an Answer Is Not Known:
1 — 2 — 3 — 4 — 5 — 6 — 7 — 8 — 9 — 10

Good Memory:
1 — 2 — 3 — 4 — 5 — 6 — 7 — 8 — 9 — 10

Does Not Offer Alibi for Shortcomings:
1 — 2 — 3 — 4 — 5 — 6 — 7 — 8 — 9 — 10

Never Blames Others for Mistakes:
1 — 2 — 3 — 4 — 5 — 6 — 7 — 8 — 9 — 10

Go-Giver:
1 — 2 — 3 — 4 — 5 — 6 — 7 — 8 — 9 — 10

Runs Successful Business:
1 — 2 — 3 — 4 — 5 — 6 — 7 — 8 — 9 — 10

Lives an Abundant Life:
1 — 2 — 3 — 4 — 5 — 6 — 7 — 8 — 9 — 10

Makes Presence Known:
1 — 2 — 3 — 4 — 5 — 6 — 7 — 8 — 9 — 10

An Inspiration to Others:
1 — 2 — 3 — 4 — 5 — 6 — 7 — 8 — 9 — 10

Strong Mind and Uses It for All Purposes:
1 — 2 — 3 — 4 — 5 — 6 — 7 — 8 — 9 — 10

Think for Yourself:
1 — 2 — 3 — 4 — 5 — 6 — 7 — 8 — 9 — 10

42. Tally your score in the twenty areas above. Your score is ____ /200.

43. Review the self-assessments you just took. Tally the percentage that you possess with each. Are you leaning more into the drifter or non-drifter category?

44. Where do you see your greatest weaknesses and best opportunities for improvement?

45. Where do you see your greatest strengths?

46. Do you believe there is a way out of the negative traits that you have and the self-destructive choices you have made thus far in your life? Please explain.

47. The Devil advises drifters to wake up and give some form of service toward others. Do you serve others? If so, how? If not, how might you start doing so?

48. The Devil asserts that you must give before you get. This can be difficult; however, it is often suggested if you want to live an abundant and successful life. Do you believe this to be true? What examples have you seen of it in your life and in the world around you?

49. At the end of this chapter the Devil states that if he tries to suppress the publication of this book, it would be the surest way to have Napoleon Hill publish it. This reflects the theory that repression breeds the opposite, and what you resist, persists. What examples of this theory have you experienced in your life? Write about at least one example.

Chapter 5

The Confession Continues

Q If this confession of yours stopped right here your statement would be sound, but fortunately for millions of your victims who will gain their release because of your confession, this interview will continue until you have supplied me with the weapon by which you will eventually be restrained from domination of people through their fears and superstitions. Remember, Your Majesty, your confession has just begun. After I wring from you a description of the methods by which you control people, I will force you also to give the formula by which your control can be broken at will.

It is true I shall not remain here long enough to defeat you, but the published word I leave behind me will be deathless because it will consist of truth! You fear the opposition of no individual because you know it will be short, but you do fear truth. You fear truth and nothing else, for the reason it is slowly but definitely giving human beings freedom from all manner of fear. Without the weapon of fear you would be helpless and entirely unable to control any human being! Is that true or false?

A. I have no alternative but to admit that what you say is true.

Q Now that we understand each other, let us go ahead with your confession. But before we continue, I may as well take time out to do a little boasting on my own account, now that you have had your fling at it. I will confine myself to one question, the answer to which will give me all the satisfaction I want. Is it not true that you control only the minds of those who have allowed the drifting habit to be fixed upon them?

A. Yes, that is true. I have already admitted this truth in a dozen or more different ways. Why do you tantalize me by repeating the question?

Q There is power in repetition. I am forcing you to repeat the highlights of your confession in as many different ways as possible so your victims may check this interview and determine its soundness by their own experiences with you. That is one of my little tricks. Do you approve of my method?

A. You couldn't be setting a trap for me for the purpose of doing some more boasting, could you?

Q I am asking the questions and you are doing the answering! Go ahead now and confess why you are powerless to stop me from forcing this confession from you. I want your confession for aid and comfort to victims of yours whom I intend to release from your control the moment they read your confession.

A. I am powerless to influence or control you because you have found the secret approach to my kingdom. You know that I exist only in the minds of people who have fears. You know that I control only the drifters who neglect to use their own minds. You know that my hell is here on earth and not in the world that comes after death. And you know also that drifters supply all the fire I use in my hell. You know that I am a principle or form of energy which expresses the negative side of matter and energy, and that I am not a person with a forked tongue and a spiked tail You have become my master because you have mastered all your fears. Lastly, you know that you can release all of my earthbound victims whom you contact, and this definite knowledge is the blow with which you will deal me the greatest damage.

I cannot control you because you have discovered your own mind and you have taken charge of it. There now, Mr. Earthbound, that confession should feed your vanity to the bursting point.

Q. That last dart was unnecessary. Knowledge of the sort I have used to master you does not contaminate itself with vulgar indulgence in vanity. Truth is the one, and only, thing in the world that can stand ridicule. Now let us continue with your confession. What is wrong with the principle of flattery? You use it, do you not?

A. Do I use it? Man alive! Flattery is one of my most useful weapons. With this deadly instrument I slay the big ones and the little ones.

Q. Your admission interests me. Go ahead now and tell me how you make use of flattery.

A. I make use of it in so many ways it is difficult to know where to begin.

I warn you, before I answer in detail, that publishing my answers will bring down an avalanche of ridicule on your head for bringing up the question.

Q. I'll take the responsibility. Proceed.

A. Well, I may as well here admit that you have stumbled onto the major secret of how I convert people to the habit of drifting!

Q. That is a startling admission. Go ahead with your confession, and stick strictly to this subject of flattery. No more side remarks and no more facetiousness for the present. Tell me all about your use of flattery in gaining control over people.

A. Flattery is a bait of incomparable value to all who wish to gain control over others. It has powerful pulling qualities because it operates through two of the most common human weaknesses: vanity and egotism. There is a certain amount of vanity and egotism in everyone. In some people these qualities are so pronounced they literally serve as a rope by which one may be bound. The best of all ropes is flattery.

Flattery is the chief bait through which men seduce women. Sometimes—in fact, frequently—women use the same bait to gain control of men, especially men who cannot be mastered through sex appeal. I teach its use to both men and women. Flattery is the chief bait with which my agents weave their way into the confidence of people from whom they procure information needed to carry on warfare.

Wherever anyone stops to feed his vanity on flattery, I move in and begin to build another drifter. Non-drifters are not easily flattered. I inspire people to use flattery in every human relationship where its use is possible because those who are influenced by it become easy victims of the drifting habit.

Q Can you control anyone who is amenable to flattery?
A. Very easily. As I have already told you, flattery is of major importance in alluring people into the habit of drifting.

Q At what age are people most susceptible to flattery?
A. Age has nothing to do with one's susceptibility to flattery. People respond to it, in one way or another, from the time they become conscious of their own existence until they die.

Q Through what motive can women be most easily flattered?
A. Their vanity. Tell a woman she is pretty or that she wears clothes well.

Q What motive is most effective in harpooning men?
A. Egotism, with a capital E! Tell a man he has a strong Herculean body or that he is a great business tycoon, and he will

purr like a cat and smile like an opossum! After that you know what happens.

Q Are all men like that?
A. Oh, no. Two out of every hundred have their egotism so thoroughly under control that even an expert flatterer couldn't get under their skins with a double-edged butcher knife.

Q How does a cunning woman apply her art of flattery in attracting men?
A. Great heavens, man, do I have to draw a picture of her method for you? Have you no imagination?

Q Oh, yes, I have imagination enough, Your Majesty, but I am thinking of the poor dupes of the world who need to understand the exact technique with which they may be flattered into the habit of drifting. Go on and tell us how a woman can harpoon rich and presumably smart men.
A. This is a devilish trick to play on women, but since you demand the information I am helpless to withhold it. Women influence men through a technique consisting, first, of ability to inject soft, cooing baby tones into their voices, and, second, by closing their eyes into a half-closed position which registers hypnotism in connection with the flattery of men.

Q Is that all there is to the business of flattery?
A. No, that is only the technique. Then comes the motive a woman uses as a lure. The type of woman you perhaps have in mind never sells a man herself or anything she can give him. Instead she sells him his own egotism!

Q Is that all that women use when they wish to flatter men?
A. That is the most effective thing they use It works when sex appeal fails!

Q So I am to believe that big, strong, smart men can be wound up and manipulated through flattery, just as if they were so much putty? Is that possible?

A. Is it possible? It is happening every minute of the day. Moreover, unless they are non-drifters, the bigger they come, the harder they fall when the expert flatterer moves in on them.

Q Tell me of some of your other tricks with which you cause people to drift in life.

A. One of my most effective devices is failure! The majority of people begin to drift as soon as they meet with opposition, and not one out of ten thousand will keep on trying after failing two or three times.

Q So it is your business to induce people to fail whenever you can. Is that correct?

A. You have it right. Failure breaks down one's morale, destroys self-confidence, subdues enthusiasm, dulls imagination, and drives away definiteness of purpose.

Without these qualities no one can permanently succeed in any undertaking. The world has produced thousands of inventors with ability superior to that of the late Thomas A. Edison. But these men have never been heard of, while the name of Edison will go marching on because Edison converted failure into a stepping stone to achievement while the others used it as an alibi for not producing results.

Q Is the capacity to surmount failure without being discouraged one of Henry Ford's chief assets?

A. Yes, and this same quality is the chief asset of every man who attains outstanding success in any calling.

Q That statement covers lots of territory, Your Majesty. Do you not wish to modify it or tone it down a bit for the sake of accuracy?

A. No modification is necessary because the claim is none too broad. Search accurately into the lives of men and women who achieve enduring success and you will find, without exception, that their success has been in exact proportion to the extent that they surmounted failure.

The life of every successful person loudly acclaims that which every true philosopher knows: "Every failure brings with it the seed of an equivalent success."

But the seed will not germinate and grow under the influence of a drifter. It springs to life only when it is in the hands of one who recognizes that most failures are only temporary defeat, and who never, under any circumstances, accepts defeat as an excuse for drifting.

Q. If I understand you correctly, you claim there is virtue in failure. That does not seem reasonable. Why do you try to induce people to fail if there is virtue in failure?

A. There is no inconsistency in my claims. The appearance of inconsistency is due to your lack of understanding. Failure is a virtue only when it does not lead one to quit trying and begin drifting. I induce as many people as I can to fail as often as possible for the reason that not one out of ten thousand will keep on trying after failing two or three times. I am not concerned about the few who convert failures into stepping stones because they belong to my opposition anyway. They are the non-drifters and therefore they are beyond my reach.

Q. Your explanation clears up the matter. Now go ahead and tell me of some of your other tricks with which you allure people into drifting.

A. One of my most effective tricks is known to you as propaganda. This is the instrument of greatest value to me in setting people to murdering one another under the guise of war.

The cleverness of this trick consists mainly of the subtlety with which I use it.

I mix propaganda with the news of the world. I have it taught in public and private schools. I see that it finds its way into the pulpit. I color moving pictures with it I see that it enters every home where there is a radio. I inject it into billboard, newspaper, and radio advertising. I spread it in every place of business where people work. I use it to fill the divorce courts and I make it serve to destroy business and industry.

It is my chief instrument for starting runs on banks. My propagandists cover the world so thoroughly that I can start epidemics of disease, turn loose the dogs of war, or throw business into a panic at will.

Q **If you can do all that you claim with propaganda, it is little wonder that we have wars and business depressions. Give me a simple description of what you mean by the term "propaganda." Just what is it and how does it work? I wish to know particularly how you cause people to drift through the use of this devilish device.**

A. Propaganda is any device, plan, or method by which people can be influenced without knowing that they are being influenced, or the source of the influence.

Propaganda is used in business for the purpose of discouraging competition. Employers use it to gain advantage over their employees. The employees retaliate by using it to gain advantage over their employers. In fact, it is used so universally and through such a smooth and beautiful streamlined technique that it looks harmless even when it is detected.

Q **I suppose some of your boys are now engaged in preparing the minds of the American people to drift into some form of dictatorship. Tell me how they work.**

A. Yes! Millions of my boys are preparing Americans to become Hitlerized. My best boys are working through politics and labor organization. We intend to take over the country with ballots instead of bullets. Americans are so sensitive they would never stand the shock of seeing their form of government changed with the aid of machine guns and tank cars. So our propaganda boys are serving them a diet they will swallow, by stirring up strife between employers and employees and turning the government against business and industry. When propaganda has done its work thoroughly, one of my boys will move in as dictator and the Nine Old Men on your Supreme Court with their silly notions of the Constitution will move out!

Everyone will be given a job or fed from the government treasury. When men's bellies are filled, they drift freely with one who does the filling. Hungry men get out from under control.

Q. I have often wondered who invented the clever trick which you call propaganda. From what you tell me of its source and nature I understand why it is so deadly. Only one as clever as Your Majesty could have invented such a device with which to dull the reason, dethrone the will, and lure men into drifting.

Why do you not use your powerful propaganda to gain control of your victims instead of subduing them through fear and annihilating them through warfare?

A. What is fear of the Devil except propaganda? You have not observed my technique very carefully or you would have seen that I am the world's greatest propagandist! I never attain an end by direct, open means which I can achieve through subterfuge and subtlety. What do you suppose I am using, when I plant negative ideas in the minds of men and gain control of them through what they believe to be their own ideas? What would you call that except the cleverest of all forms of propaganda?

Q. Surely you are not going to tell me that you destroy people through their own help without their realizing what you are doing?

A. That is exactly what I wish you to understand. Moreover, I will show you exactly how the trick is performed.

Q Now we are getting somewhere. Exactly how do you convert human beings into propagandists and lure them into self-imprisonment? Give me the story with all its lurid details. This is the most important part of your confession and I am consumed with eagerness to gain control of your secret. I can hardly blame you for stalling about answering my question because you know so well that your answer will snatch millions of innocent victims from your control. You also know that your answer will protect other countless millions of yet unborn people from being victimized by you. It is little wonder you are hedging about answering.

A. Your deductions are correct. This part of my confession will do me more damage than all the remainder of it.

Q Stating your headache in a better way, this part of your confession will save more millions of people from your control than all the remainder of it.

A. All I can say is that you have me in a hell of a situation!

Q Now you shall know how the millions of your victims feel. Let's have it.

A. I make my first entry into an individual's mind by bribing him.

Q What do you use as a bribe?

A. I use many things, all of them pleasant things the individual covets. I use the same sort of bribes that individuals use when they bribe one another. That is, I use for bribes the things people most want. My best bribes are these:
- Love
- The thirst for sex expression
- Covetousness for money
- The obsessive desire to gain something for nothing—gambling
- Vanity in women, egotism in men
- Desire to be the master of others
- Desire for intoxicants and narcotics

- Desire for self-expression through words and deeds
- Desire to imitate others
- Desire for perpetuation of life after death
- Desire to be a hero or heroine
- Desire for physical food

Q That is an imposing list of bribes, Your Majesty. Do you use others?

A. Yes, plenty of them, but these are my favorites. Through some combination of them I can enter the mind of any human being at will at any age from birth until death.

Q You mean that these bribes are the keys with which you can silently unlock the door to any mind you choose?

A. That is exactly what I mean and I can do it too.

Q What happens when you enter the mind of a person who is not yet in the habit of drifting, but belongs in the 98 percent class as a potential drifter?

A. I go to work immediately to occupy as much of that person's mind as I can master. If the individual's greatest weakness is the desire for money, I begin to dangle coins before him, figuratively speaking. I intensify his desire and induce him to go after money. Then when he gets near it I snatch it away from him.

This is an old trick of mine. After the trick has been repeated a few times, the poor fellow gives in and quits. Then I take over a little more space in his mind and fill it with the fear of poverty. That is one of my best mind-fillers.

Q Yes, I admit your method is very clever, but what happens if the victim fools you and gets his hands on a lot of money? You don't fill his mind with fear of poverty then, do you?

A. No, I don't. I take over the space by filling it with something which serves my purpose just as well. If my victim converts his desire for money into large sums, I start over-feeding him with the things he can buy with it. For example, I cause him to stuff himself with rich foods. This slows down his thinking capacity, endangers his heart, and starts him on the road to drifting.

Then I pester him with intestinal poisoning through the surplus food he eats. That also slows down his thinking and gives him a nasty disposition.

Q. What if the victim is not a glutton? What other follies can you induce him to pick up that lead to drifting?

A. If the victim is a male I can usually snare him through his sex appetite.

Over-indulgence in sex starts more men to drifting toward failure than all other causes combined.

Q. So food and sex are two of your sure-fire baits! Is that correct?

A. Yes. With these two lures I can take over a majority of my victims, and then there is the desire for money.

Q. I am beginning to think that wealth is more dangerous than poverty, if your story is to be believed.

A. That altogether depends upon who has the wealth and how it was acquired.

Q. What has the manner in which money is acquired to do with its being a blessing or a curse?

A. Everything. If you don't believe me, take a look at those who acquire a large amount of money quickly, without time to get wisdom along with it, and observe how they use it.

Why, do you suppose, rich men's sons seldom equal the achievements of their fathers? I'll tell you why. It is because they have been deprived of the self-discipline which comes from being forced to work.

Look into the records of moving picture stars or athletes who suddenly find themselves in possession of big money and hero worship and praise from the public. Observe how quickly I move in and take them over in many cases, mainly through sex, gambling, food, and liquor. With these I catch and control the biggest and the best of people as soon as they get their hands on big money.

Q What about those who acquire money slowly, by rendering some form of useful service? Are they easily snared too?

A. Oh, I get them all right, but I generally have to change my bait. Some of them want one thing and others want something else.

Where my purpose is best served I see to it that they get what they want most, but I manage to wrap in the package something they don't want. The thing I give them is the definite thing that makes them drifters. Do you see how I work?

Q And very clever work it is. You lure people on through their natural desires, but you slip your deadly poison into the object of those desires wherever you can.

A. Now you are catching on. You see, I play both ends against the middle, so to speak.

Q From all you say I infer that you cannot induce a non-drifter to help you gain control of his mind by baiting him with your bribes. Is that correct?

A. That is exactly correct. I can—and I do—interest non-drifters in my bribes, because I use for the purpose of bribery the things all people naturally desire, but the non-drifter resembles a fish that steals the bait from your hook but refuses to take the hook.

The non-drifter takes from life whatever he wants, but he takes it on his own terms. The drifter takes whatever he can get, but he takes what he gets on my terms.

Stating the matter in another way, the non-drifter borrows money from a legitimate banker, if he wants it, and pays a legitimate rate of interest. The drifter goes to the pawn shop, hocks his watch, and pays a suicidal rate of interest for his loan.

Q So I draw from your claims the conclusion that your hand is mixed up somehow in all of people's troubles and miseries, even though your presence may not be visible?

A. My unwilling workers are often my best workers. You see, my unwilling workers are those whom I cannot control with some combination of bribes, people whom I have to master by fear or through some form of misfortune.

They do not wish to serve me, but they cannot avoid it because they are eternally bound to me by the habit of drifting.

Q Now I am beginning to better understand your technique. You bribe your victims through their natural desires and lead them astray while you induce them to become drifters if they respond to your lure. If they refuse to respond, you plant the seed of fear in their minds or trap them through some form of misfortune, and hog-tie them while they are down. Is that your method?

A. That is exactly the way I work. Clever, don't you think?

Q Which do you prefer to serve as your propagandists—the young or the old?

A. The young, of course! They can be influenced by most bribes more easily than people of mature judgment. Moreover, they have longer to remain in my service.

Q Your Majesty has given me a clear description of drifting. Tell me what must be done to insure against the habit of drifting. I want a complete formula that anyone can use.

A. Protection against drifting lies within easy reach of every human being who has a normal body and a sound mind. The self-defense can be applied through these simple methods:

> 1. Do your own thinking on all occasions. The fact that human beings are given complete control over nothing save the power to think their own thoughts is laden with significance.

2. Decide definitely what you want from life; then create a plan for attaining it and be willing to sacrifice everything else, if necessary, rather than accept permanent defeat.

3. Analyze temporary defeat, no matter of what nature or cause, and extract from it the seed of an equivalent advantage.

4. Be willing to render useful service equivalent to the value of all material things you demand of life, and render the service first.

5. Recognize that your brain is a receiving set that can be attuned to receive communications from the universal storehouse of Infinite Intelligence, to help you transmute your desires into their physical equivalent.

6. Recognize that your greatest asset is time, the only thing except the power of thought which you own outright, and the one thing which can be shaped into whatever material things you want. Budget your time so none of it is wasted.

7. Recognize the truth that fear generally is a filler with which the Devil occupies the unused portion of your mind. It is only a state of mind which you can control by filling the space it occupies with faith in your ability to make life provide you with whatever you demand of it.

8. When you pray, do not beg! Demand what you want and insist upon getting exactly that, with no substitutes.

9. Recognize that life is a cruel taskmaster and that either you master it or it masters you. There is no half-way or compromising point. Never accept from life anything you

do not want. If that which you do not want is temporarily forced upon you, you can refuse, in your own mind, to accept it and it will make way for the thing you do want.

10. Lastly, remember that your dominating thoughts attract, through a definite law of nature, by the shortest and most convenient route, their physical counterpart. Be careful what your thoughts dwell upon.

Q That list looks imposing. Give me a simple formula, combining all the ten points. If you had to combine all ten in one, what would it be?

A. Be definite in everything you do and never leave unfinished thoughts in the mind. Form the habit of reaching definite decisions on all subjects.

Q Can the habit of drifting be broken, or does it become permanent once it has been formed?

A. The habit can be broken if the victim has enough will power, providing it is done in time. There is a point beyond which the habit can never be broken. Beyond that point the victim is mine. He resembles a fly that has been caught in a spider's web. He may struggle, but he cannot get out. Each move he makes entangles him more securely. The web in which I entangle my victims permanently is a law of nature not yet isolated by, or understood by, men of science.

STUDY GUIDE

Chapter 5:
The Confession Continues

1. Napoleon Hill opens this chapter emphasizing that the Devil fears truth, and this fact will give humans freedom from their fears as the Devil's plans are revealed. This is reflective of the saying, "The truth will set you free." Do you believe this to be so? Please explain.

2. If you believe the previous tenet, give an example of it in your life. If not, give an example of how the truth has created negative, irreparable consequences in your life.

3. Napoleon Hill reemphasizes that the Devil controls the minds of those who have allowed the drifting habit (lack of focus, procrastination) to be fixed upon them. List at least three individuals you know who have allowed procrastination or lack of focus to get in the way of living their life dreams.

4. Repetition of the message is an effective way of teaching a new way. What have you read in this book thus far that bears repetition?

5. The Devil confesses that he only exists in the minds of those who have fears. Do an honest evaluation of yourself and list each fear that you currently have.

6. Now list each fear that you previously had but have since overcome.

7. As you reflect on the last two questions, do you believe you can overcome any fear that comes your way? Why or why not?

8. The Devil defines himself as "a principle form of energy which expresses the negative side of matter and energy, that is not a person with a forked tongue and a spiked tail." Why do you think humankind has personified the Devil in human form? What purpose would doing so serve?

9. How do you think the masses would shift if they all fully embraced this reality to be true. Write a detailed description of how you believe this

world could change if fear of the Devil as a "being or entity" did not exist.

10. Napoleon Hill states that vanity cannot contaminate truth. Explain what you believe him to mean by this statement.

11. The Devil uses flattery to gain control over people. He lists vanity and egotism as two of the most common human weaknesses. It can "serve as a rope by which one may be bound." Do you believe yourself to be bound by your own vanity? Why or why not? Please explain.

12. The Devil states that flattery is the chief bait through which information is procured to carry on warfare. What evidence of this do you see in history and now on the earth?

13. The Devil further asserts that he can control anyone who is amenable to flattery. It is difficult not to succumb to flattery. Have you found ways not to, or have you witnessed others who have? If so, please describe them.

14. Perhaps this book is showing its age with the statement that a woman can be most easily flattered by being told that she is pretty or that she wears clothes well. Why do you believe that women today may find that statement offensive? Do you believe that this shift in perception has come about through the nondrifting intentions and actions of various women since Napoleon's time in the 1930s? Please explain and provide examples.

15. The Devil asserts that men's egos are stroked when they are told that they have a "strong Herculean body or that they are a great business tycoon." Depiction of the comic strip world of strong Herculean men and women has become a box office phenomenon. Do you believe this popularity is rooted in egoic projections, or is there more to it? Please explain.

16. The Devil describes the ways in which women influence men through injecting softness by using "cooing baby tones into their voices" and by "closing their eyes into a half-closed position which registers hypnotism." When first read, this may seem odd and offensive. If you are able, step back and look for the learning opportunity in this statement. In whatever means you use, take an inventory of how you flatter others? List them.

17. How has flattery affected your life? Have you ever found yourself lost in your ego self-praise? If so, do you believe it was detrimental to your well-being? Please explain.

18. The Devil asserts that many people begin to drift when they meet with failure and opposition. He states that tens of thousands of people will give up trying after failing two or three times. Reflect on the efforts you have made throughout your life. Focusing on the perceived failures, did you give up after two or three tries? Write about your experience with apparent failures.

19. The Devil states that failure does the following:
    - Breaks down one's morale
    - Destroys self-confidence
    - Subdues enthusiasm
    - Dulls imagination
    - Drives away definiteness of purpose

    Reflect on your life. Have you experienced any of these symptoms? If so, were they in response to an apparent failure? Please explain.

20. Has anything shifted in your perception of your failures throughout the years, or have they remained constant? Did you learn anything from them? Please explain.

21. According to the Devil, Edison converted failure into a stepping-stone to achievement. Write about one instance in which you have achieved this in your life.

22. The capacity to surmount failure without being discouraged is an asset that Napoleon Hill attributes to Henry Ford. On a scale from 1 to 10 (1 being "very little" and 10 being "very much so"), rate the degree to which you believe you have been able to surmount failure in your life:

    1 —— 2 —— 3 —— 4 —— 5 —— 6 —— 7 —— 8 —— 9 —— 10

23. On a scale from 1 to 10 (1 being "very little" and 10 being "very much so"), rate the degree to which you believe you have the capacity to surmount failure in your life:

    1 —— 2 —— 3 —— 4 —— 5 —— 6 —— 7 —— 8 —— 9 —— 10

24. The adage "failure is a virtue" is referenced in this interview. How do you see this to be so in your life? If not, why not?

25. The Devil defines propaganda as "any device, plan, or method by which people can be influenced without knowing that they are being influenced, or the source of the influence." Do you believe that you and the masses can unknowingly be influenced by propaganda today?

26. The conversation moves to the area of propaganda as "the instrument . . . in setting people to murdering one another under the guise of war." It is used in all forms of media and communication. How do you currently see propaganda being used in the messages shared in the media (news, television, movies, social media, as examples) today?

27. The Devil claims that his propagandists "cover the world so thoroughly that I can start epidemics of disease, turn loose the dogs of war, or throw business into a panic at will." Do you believe that propaganda started the spread of AIDS or the COVID epidemic? Please explain.

28. Do you believe there is a way to disallow negative, fear-based propaganda in your life and in the lives of others? If so, how? If not, then do you believe that we are doomed to the fate that such powerful communication commands of the world?

29. According to the Devil, millions of boys are preparing Americans to become Hitlerized. They intend to take over the country "with ballots instead of bullets." He continues by stating that he does this by "stirring up strife between employers and employees." Do you see this being done today in America? If so, how? If not, how have we avoided it?

30. He further claims to Hitlerize America by turning the government against business and industry. Do you see this being played out in America today? If so, how? If not, how do you think America has avoided this trap?

31. The Devil goes on to assert that "when propaganda has done its work thoroughly, one of my boys will move in as a dictator and the Nine Old Men on your Supreme Court with their silly notions of the Constitution will move out!" Do you see this potentially being played out in American politics today? Please explain.

32. The Devil goes on to say that "everyone will be given a job or fed from the government treasury. When men's bellies are filled, they drift freely with one who does the filling." This appears to discourage socialized care for Americans. Do you believe this to be true? Why or why not?

33. The Devil deemed himself as the world's greatest propagandist. List at least three other propagandists that you believe have been extremely powerful in instilling fear in the world and in America, in particular.

34. The Devil confesses that he makes his first entry into people's minds by bribing them. He lists twelve desires that he manipulates to create drifters among humankind. Do an honest inner inventory. List which of the following desires you experience or have experienced in your life:
    - The thirst for sex expression (yes/no)
    - Covetousness for money (yes/no)
    - Obsessive desire to gain something for nothing (yes/no)
    - Vanity (yes/no)
    - Egotism (yes/no)
    - Desiring to be the master of others (yes/no)
    - Desire for intoxicants and narcotics (yes/no)
    - Desire for self-expression through words and deeds (yes/no)
    - Desire to imitate others (yes/no)
    - Desire for perpetuation of life after death (yes/no)
    - Desire to be a hero or heroine (yes/no)
    - Desire for physical food (yes/no)

35. Of the twelve desires listed, how many have you felt compelled by at some time in your life?

36. Do you believe that the list is accurate and complete? Are there any desires that have compelled you that were not listed? If so, list them.

37. Napoleon Hill asks the Devil what happens when he enters the mind of a person who is not yet in the habit of drifting. He asserts that he draws the individual closer to their goal and then, once close to attaining it, he snatches it away from them. Have you noted a situation in your life where you were close to attaining a goal, only to find it "snatched" away?

38. The Devil shares that one challenge for many is the acquisition of money quickly and without the discipline and the time to get wisdom along with it. This is often said to be true of lottery winners, for example. Provide an example of such a situation, either in your life or in the life of someone who was covered in the media.

39. The Devil states that "the nondrifter takes from life whatever he wants, but he takes it on his own terms. The drifter takes whatever he can get, but he takes what he gets on my terms." Based on this insight, do you see yourself as a potential drifter or nondrifter?

40. The Devil prefers to use youthful individuals as his propagandists because they most often tend to lack the judgment of someone older. Do you see this reflected in the world today? If so, how?

41. There are several actions that are listed which can be taken to ensure against the habit of drifting. Review the list and rate your current state with each (1 being "very little" and 10 being "very much so"):

Do your own thinking on all occasions.

1 —— 2 —— 3 —— 4 —— 5 —— 6 —— 7 —— 8 —— 9 —— 10

Make a definite decision of what you want from life, then create a plan and be willing to sacrifice all rather than accept defeat.

1 —— 2 —— 3 —— 4 —— 5 —— 6 —— 7 —— 8 —— 9 —— 10

Analyze temporary defeat and find the seed of equivalent advantage from it.

1 —— 2 —— 3 —— 4 —— 5 —— 6 —— 7 —— 8 —— 9 —— 10

Serve others first, and to the equivalent value of your material demands.

1 —— 2 —— 3 —— 4 —— 5 —— 6 —— 7 —— 8 —— 9 —— 10

Recognize your brain as a receptor of Infinite Universal Intelligence that helps you to transmute and manifest your desires.

1 —— 2 —— 3 —— 4 —— 5 —— 6 —— 7 —— 8 —— 9 —— 10

See time as your greatest asset, and budget it accordingly.

1 —— 2 —— 3 —— 4 —— 5 —— 6 —— 7 —— 8 —— 9 —— 10

Recognize fear as a filler of the unused part of your mind that you can control through faith in your abilities.

1 —— 2 —— 3 —— 4 —— 5 —— 6 —— 7 —— 8 —— 9 —— 10

When praying, do not beg but demand what you want and insist upon it.

1 —— 2 —— 3 —— 4 —— 5 —— 6 —— 7 —— 8 —— 9 —— 10

Master life before it masters you and do not compromise on what you want.

1 —— 2 —— 3 —— 4 —— 5 —— 6 —— 7 —— 8 —— 9 —— 10

Remember that your Dominating Thoughts attract via the law of nature. Be careful of what your thoughts dwell upon.

1 —— 2 —— 3 —— 4 —— 5 —— 6 —— 7 —— 8 —— 9 —— 10

42. To encapsulate this message, "Be definite in everything you do and never leave unfinished thoughts in the mind. Form the habit of reaching definite decisions on all subjects." What message would your "other self" give you as far as how you are currently living this practice?

43. This chapter ends with the encouragement that the habit of drifting can be broken if done in time. Do you believe you are on the right track? If not, do you believe there is still time to shift from fear to faith in your life? If not, could your hopelessness be a trap to discourage you from imminent success in your life. Take some time to reflect and write about any insights you gain from doing so.

Chapter 6

Hypnotic Rhythm

Q What is this mysterious law through which you take permanent control of people's bodies even before you take over their souls? The whole world will want to know more about this law and how it operates.

A. It will be hard to describe the law so you will understand it, but you may call it "hypnotic rhythm." It is the same law through which people can be hypnotized.

Q So you have the power to use the laws of nature as a web in which you bind your victims in eternal control. Is that your claim?

A. That is not only my claim. It is the truth! I take over their minds and bodies even before they die whenever I can lure them or frighten them into hypnotic rhythm.

Q What is hypnotic rhythm? How do you use it to gain permanent mastery over human beings?

A. I will have to go back into time and space and give you a brief elementary description of how nature uses hypnotic rhythm. Otherwise you will not be able to understand my description of how I use this universal law to control human beings.

Q. Go ahead, but keep your story confined to simple illustrations which come within the range of my own experience and knowledge of natural laws.

A. Very well, I shall do my best. You, of course, know that nature maintains a perfect balance between all the elements and all the energy in the universe. You can see that the stars and the planets move with perfect precision, each one keeping its own place in time and space. You can see that the seasons of the year come and go with perfect regularity. You can see that an oak tree grows from an acorn and a pine grows from the seed of its ancestor. An acorn never produces a pine and a pine seed never produces an oak.

These are simple things which anyone can understand; what one cannot see is the universal law through which nature maintains perfect balance throughout the myriad of universes.

You earthbound caught a fragmentary glimpse of this great universal law when Newton discovered that it holds your earth in its position and causes all material objects to be attracted toward the center of the earth. He called the law gravitation.

But he did not go far enough in his study of the law. If he had, he would have discovered that the same law which holds your earth in position and helps nature to maintain a perfect balance over the four dimensions—in which all matter and energy are contained— is the web in which I entangle and control the minds of human beings.

Q. Tell me more of this astounding law of hypnotic rhythm.

A. As I have already stated, there is a universal form of energy with which nature keeps a perfect balance between all matter and energy. She makes specialized use of this universal building material by breaking it up into different wavelengths. The breaking-up process is carried on through habit.

You will better understand what I am trying to convey if I compare it with the method by which one learns to play music. At first the notes are memorized in the mind. Then they are related to one another through melody and rhythm. By repetition the melody and rhythm become fixed in the mind. Observe how relentlessly the musician must repeat a tune before he masters it. Through repetition the musical notes blend and then you have music.

Any impulse of thought that the mind repeats over and over through habit forms an organized rhythm. Undesirable habits can be broken. They must be broken before they assume the proportions of rhythm. Are you following me?

Q. Yes.
A. Well, to continue, rhythm is the last stage of habit! Any thought or physical movement which is repeated over and over through the principle of habit finally reaches the proportion of rhythm.

Then the habit cannot be broken because nature takes it over and makes it permanent. It is something like a whirlpool in water. An object may keep floating indefinitely unless it is caught in a whirlpool. Then it is carried round and round but it cannot escape. The energy with which people think may be compared with water in a river.

Q. So this is the way in which you take control of the minds of people, is it?
A. Yes. All I have to do to gain control over any mind is to induce its owner to drift.

Q. Am I to understand that the habit of drifting is the major danger through which people lose their prerogative or privilege of thinking their own thoughts and shaping their own earthly destinations?
A. That and much more. Drifting is also the habit through which I take over their souls after they give up their physical bodies.

Q. Then the only way a human being can be saved from eternal annihilation is by maintaining control over his own mind while he is on this earth. Is that true?

A. You have stated the truth perfectly! Those who control and use their own minds escape my web. I get all the others as naturally as the sun sets in the west.

Q. Is that all there is to the business of being saved from eternal annihilation? Doesn't what you call your opposition have anything to do with saving people?

A. I can see that you do think very deeply. My opposition—the power you earthbound call God—has everything to do with the salvation of people from eternal annihilation, and for that reason it is my opposition who provides every human being with the privilege of using his own mind.

If you use that power by maintaining control over your own mind, you become a part of it when you give up your physical body. If you neglect to use it, then I have the privilege of taking advantage of the neglect through the law of hypnotic rhythm.

Q. How much of a person do you take over when you gain control of him?

A. Everything that is left after he ceases to control and use his own mind.

Q. In other words, when you gain control of a person you take over all there is of his individuality up to the time that he quits using his own mind. Is that correct?

A. That is how I operate.

Q. What do you do with people whom you control before death? Of what good are they to you while they live?

A. I use them, or what is left of than after I take charge, as propagandists to help me prepare the minds of others to drift.

Q You not only fool people into destroying their power to control their own minds, but you use them to help you trap others?
A. Yes, I let no opportunity get away from me.

Q Let us come back to the subject of hypnotic rhythm. Tell me more of how this law works. Show me how you use individuals to help you gain control over others. I want to know something of the most effective way you use hypnotic rhythm.

A. Oh, that is easy! The thing I like best is to fill the minds of people with fear. Once I fill one's mind with fear I have little trouble causing him to drift until I have entangled him in the web of hypnotic rhythm.

Q What human fear best serves your purpose?
A. The fear of death.

Q Why is the fear of death your favorite weapon?
A. Because no one knows, and by the very nature of the laws of the universe, no one can prove definitely what happens after death. This uncertainty frightens people out of their wits.

People who give over their minds to fear—any sort of fear neglect to use their minds and begin to drift. Eventually they drift into the whirlpool of hypnotic rhythm from which they may never escape.

Q Then you do not mind what religious leaders think or say of you when they speak of death?
A. Not as long as they say something! If the churches should stop talking about me, my cause would receive a severe setback. Every attack made against me fixes the fear of me in the minds of all who are influenced by it. You see, opposition is the thing that keeps some people from drifting!
Providing they do not yield to it.

Q Since you claim the churches help instead of hindering your cause, tell me what would give you cause to worry?

A. My only worry is that someday a real thinker may appear on earth.

Q What would happen if a thinker did appear?

A. You ask me what would happen? I'll tell you what would happen.

People would learn the greatest of all truths—that the time they spend in fearing something would, if reversed, give them all they want in the material world and save them from me after death. Isn't that worth thinking about?

Q What is keeping such a thinker from appearing in the world?

A. Fear of criticism! It may interest you to know that the fear of criticism is the only effective weapon I have with which to whip you. If you were not afraid to publish this confession after you wring it from me, I would lose my earthly kingdom.

Q And if I did surprise you and publish it, how long would it be until you lost your kingdom?

A. Just long enough for one generation of children to grow into understanding. You cannot take the adults from me. I have them too securely sewed up. But if you published this confession, it would be sufficient to keep me from gaining control of the yet unborn and those who have not yet reached the age of reason. You wouldn't dare publish what I have told you about the religious leaders. They would crucify you!

Q I thought the savage practice of crucifixion went out of style two thousand years ago.

A. I don't mean crucifixion on a cross. I mean social and financial crucifixion. Your income would be shut off. You would become a social outcast. Religious leaders and their followers alike would treat you with scorn.

Q Suppose I should choose to throw in my lot with the select few who make a pretense of using their own minds rather than fear the masses who do not—the masses of whom you claim 98 percent?

A. If you have courage enough to do this, you will crimp my style.

Q Why do you lay claim to no scientist? Don't you like scientists?

A. Oh yes, I like all people well enough, but true scientists are out of my reach.

Q Why?

A. Because they think for themselves and spend their time studying natural laws. They deal with cause and effect. They deal with facts wherever they find them. But do not make the mistake of believing scientists have no religion. They have a very definite religion.

Q What is their religion?

A. The religion of truth! The religion of natural law! If the world ever produces an accurate thinker with ability to fathom the deeply buried secret of life and death, you can be sure that science will be responsible for the catastrophe.

Q Catastrophe to whom?

A. To me, of course!

Q Let's get back to the subject of hypnotic rhythm. I want to know more about it. Is it something like the principle through which people can hypnotize one another?

A. It is precisely the same thing. I have already told you so. Why do you repeat your questions?

Q That is an old worldly custom of mine, Your Majesty. For your enlightenment I will tell you I am forcing you to repeat many of your statements for the sake of emphasis. I am also trying to see if I can catch you in a lie! Don't dodge the issue. Get back to hypnotic rhythm and tell me all you know about it. Am I a victim of it?

A. Not now, but you barely missed falling into my web. You drifted toward the whirlpool of hypnotic rhythm, until you discovered how to force me into making this confession. Then I lost control of you!

Q How interesting. You are not trying to recapture me through flattery, are you?

A. That would be the best bribe I could offer you. It is the bribe I used on you effectively before you got the upper hand of me.

Q With what did you flatter me?

A. With many things, chief among them sex and the desire for self-expression.

Q What effect did your bribes have on me?

A. They caused you to neglect your major purpose in life and started you to drifting.

Q Was that all you did to me through your bribes?

A. That was plenty.

Q But I am back on the track and out of your reach now, am I not?

A. Yes, you are temporarily out of my reach because you are not drifting.

Q What broke your spell over me and released me from the habit of drifting?

A. My answer may humiliate you. Do you want to hear it?

Q Go ahead and give it to me, Your Majesty. I wish to learn how much truth I can stand.
A. When you found a great love in the woman of your choice, I lost my grip on you.

Q So you are going to accuse me of hiding behind a woman's skirts, are you?
A. No, not hiding. I wouldn't put it that way. I would say you have learned how to give yourself a solid background with the embellishment of a woman's mind.

Q The woman's skirt has nothing to do with it then?
A. No, but her brain does. When you and your wife began to combine your two brains, through your habit of "Master Minding" every day, you stumbled upon the secret power with which you forced me into this confession.

Q Is that the truth, or are you trying to flatter me again?
A. I could flatter you if I had you alone, but I cannot flatter you while you have the use of your wife's mind.

Q I am beginning to catch on to something important. I am beginning to understand what was meant by the writer of that passage in the Bible which says substantially, "When two or more meet together and ask for anything in My name, it shall be granted." It is true, then, that two minds are better than one.
A. It is not only true, it is necessary before anyone can continuously contact the great storehouse of Infinite Intelligence wherein is stored all that is, all that ever was, and all that can ever be.

Q Is there such a storehouse?
A. If there had not been, you would not—could not—now be humiliating me with this silly forced confession.

Q Isn't it dangerous to give this sort of information to the world?
A. Sure, it is dangerous to me. If I were you, I would not give it out.

Q Let us get back, now, to the technique through which you fasten on your victims the habit of drifting. What is the very first step a drifter must take to break the habit?
A. A burning desire to break it! You of course know that no one can be hypnotized by another person without his willingness to be hypnotized. The willingness may assume the form of indifference toward life generally, lack of ambition, fear, lack of definiteness of purpose, and many other forms. Nature does not need one's consent in order to place him under the spell of hypnotic rhythm. It needs only to find him off guard, through any form of neglect to use his own mind. Remember this: whatever you have, you use it or you lose it!

All successful attempts to break the habit of drifting must be done before nature makes the habit permanent, through hypnotic rhythm.

Q As I understand you, hypnotic rhythm is a natural law through which nature fixes the vibration of all environments. Is that true?
A. Yes, nature uses hypnotic rhythm to make one's dominating thoughts and one's thought-habits permanent. That is why poverty is disease. Nature makes it so by fixing permanently the thought-habits of all who accept poverty as an unavoidable circumstance.

Through this same law of hypnotic rhythm, nature will also fix permanently positive thoughts of opulence and prosperity.

Perhaps you will better understand the working principle of hypnotic rhythm if I tell you its nature is to fix permanently all habits whether they are mental or physical. If your mind fears poverty, your mind will attract poverty. If your mind demands opulence and expects it, your mind will attract the physical and financial equivalents of opulence. This is in accordance with an immutable law of nature.

Q Did the writer of that sentence in the Bible, "Whatsoever a man soweth, that shall he also reap," have in mind this law of nature?

A. He could have nothing else in mind. The statement is true. You can see evidence of its truth in all human relationships.

Q And that is why the man who forms the habit of drifting through life must accept whatever life hands him. Is that correct?

A. That is absolutely correct. Life pays the drifter its own price, on its own terms. The non-drifter makes life pay on his own terms.

Q Doesn't the question of morals enter into what one gets from life?

A. To be sure, but only for the reason that one's morals have an influence on one's thoughts. No one can collect what he wants from life merely by being good, if that is what you want to know.

Q No, I guess not. I see what you mean. We are all where we are and what we are because of our own deeds.

A. No, not exactly. You are where you are and what you are because of your thoughts and your deeds.

Q Then there is no such reality as luck, is there?

A. Emphatically no. Circumstances which people do not understand are classified under the heading of luck. Back of every reality is a cause. Often the cause is so far removed from the effect that the circumstance can be explained only by attributing it to the operation of luck. Nature knows no such law as luck. It is a man-made hypothesis with which he explains away things he does not understand. The terms "luck" and "miracle" are twin sisters. Neither of them has any real existence except in the imaginations of people. Both are used to explain that which people do not understand.

Remember this: everything having a real existence is capable of proof. Keep this one truth in mind and you will become a sounder thinker.

Q Which is more important, one's thoughts or one's deeds?
A. All deeds follow thoughts. There can be no deeds without their having first been patterned in thought. Moreover, all thoughts have a tendency to clothe themselves in their physical counterpart. One's dominating thoughts, that is, the thoughts one mixes with the emotions, desire, hope, faith, fear, hate, greed, enthusiasm, not only have a tendency to clothe themselves in their physical equivalent, but they are bound to do so.

Q That reminds me to ask you to tell me more about yourself. Where, in addition to the minds of people, do you dwell and operate?
A. I operate wherever there is something I can control and appropriate. I have already told you I am the negative portion of the electron of matter.

- I am the explosion in lightning.
- I am the pain in disease and physical suffering.
- I am the unseen general in warfare.
- I am the unknown commissioner of poverty and famine.
- I am the executioner extraordinaire at death.
- I am the inspirer of lust after the flesh.
- I am the creator of jealousy and envy and greed.
- I am the instigator of fear.
- I am the genius who converts the achievements of men of science into instruments of death.
- I am the destroyer of harmony in all manner of human relationships.
- I am the antithesis of justice.

- I am the driving force in all immorality.
- I am the stalemate of all good.
- I am anxiety, suspense, superstition, and insanity.
- I am the destroyer of hope and faith.
- I am the inspirer of destructive gossip and scandal.
- I am the discourager of free and independent thought.
- In brief, I am the creator of all forms of human misery, the instigator of discouragement and disappointment.

Q And you do not call that cold and cruel?
A. I call that definite and dependable.
The world depression broke up the habits of men everywhere and redistributed the sources of opportunity in all walks of life on an unprecedented scale.

The drifter's pet alibi, with which he tries to explain away his undesirable position, is his cry that the world has run dry of opportunities.

Non-drifters do not wait for opportunity to be placed in their way. They create opportunity to fit their desires and demands of life!

Q Are non-drifters smart enough to avoid the influence of hypnotic rhythm?
A. No one is smart enough to dodge the influence of hypnotic rhythm.

One could just as easily avoid the influence of the law of gravity. The law of hypnotic rhythm fixes permanently the dominating thoughts of men, whether they be drifters or non-drifters.

There is no reason why a non-drifter would want to avoid the influence of hypnotic rhythm, because that law is favorable to him. It helps him convert his dominating aims, plans, and purposes into their physical replicas. It fixes his habits of thought and makes them permanent.

Only the drifter would wish to dodge the influence of hypnotic rhythm.

Q For the better portion of my adult life I have been a drifter. How did I manage to escape being swept into the whirlpool of hypnotic rhythm?

A. You haven't escaped. The major portion of your dominating thoughts and desires, since you reached adulthood, has been a well-defined, definite desire to understand all the potentialities of the mind.

You may have drifted on thoughts of lesser importance, but you did not drift in connection with this desire. Because you did not drift, you are now recording a document which gives you exactly what your dominating thoughts demanded of life.

Q Why doesn't your opposition use hypnotic rhythm to make permanent one's higher thoughts and nobler deeds? Why does your opposition permit you to use this stupendous force as a means of entangling people in a web of evil spun by their own thoughts and deeds? Why does your opposition not outwit you by binding people with thoughts which build and lift them above your influence?

A. The law of hypnotic rhythm is available to all who will use it. I make use of it more effectively than does my opposition because I offer people more attractive bribes to think my sort of thoughts and indulge in my sort of deeds.

Q In other words, you control people by making negative thinking and destructive deeds pleasing to them. Is that correct?

A. That is the idea, exactly!

STUDY GUIDE

Chapter 6:
Hypnotic Rhythm

1. Have you heard of hypnotic rhythm? If so, please explain. If not, research and write about your findings.

2. The analogy used for describing hypnotic rhythm is a whirlpool of water. Once an object is caught in the whirlpool, it cannot escape. Similarly, Napoleon concludes that the only way individuals can escape the web of hypnotic rhythm is to control and use their minds. Have you ever found yourself caught in a web of negative thoughts from which you cannot escape? If so, explain.

3. The Devil claims that when you use your mind, you become part of it at the time of your death. If not, he takes you over through hypnotic rhythm. Do you think that this could be possible, Why or why not?

4. The Devil shares that humankind's fear of death is his favorite weapon. He further explains that if the churches stopped talking about him, his cause would receive a severe setback. Do you believe this to be true? Why or why not?

5. The Devil claims that if a real thinker was to appear on the earth, he would be rendered powerless. He claims that fear of criticism is keeping such a thinker from appearing. Do you believe this to be possible?

6. Do you think that there are currently real thinkers on this earth who do not speak out because they fear criticism?

7. Do you know of any real thinkers who are speaking out?

8. The Devil claims not to focus on scientists because their religion is truth and natural law. With such laws there is no room for manipulation and perpetuating false fear. Do you believe this to be true? Why or why not?

9. The Devil claimed to have almost captured Napoleon Hill through sex and the desire for self-expression. They almost caused him to neglect

his major purpose in life. Ultimately the Devil shared that he lost his grip on Napoleon when he found great love in his wife. Do you have a life partner? If so, do you believe they raise you out of negative thinking and into a more positive, fearless place? Please explain. If you do not have a life partner, do you think having one would lift you out of fearful thinking? Why or why not?

10. The Devil claimed that Napoleon and his wife stumbled upon the secret power of Master Minding that ultimately forced him into the confession he was making in this book. Do you or have you ever practiced Master Minding? If so, what was your experience? If not, would you ever consider it? Why or why not?

11. According to the Devil, the joining of two minds is necessary for continuous contact with the great storehouse of Infinite Intelligence. Do you find greater energy and connection when involving another in that for which you are focusing in your life?

12. The first step a drifter must take to break a habit is "a burning desire to break it." Do you currently have a burning desire to break any self-destructive or negative habits? If so, list them. If not, why not?

13. The Devil goes on to warn in relation to the mind that "whatever you have, you use it, or you lose it." Do you actively work toward using and challenging your mind? If so, list how. If not, how might you start to do so?

14. According to the Devil, once habits are repeated long enough, through hypnotic rhythm they can become permanent. Are there any negative or self-destructive habits that you have for which you are concerned could become permanent? If so, list them.

15. Hypnotic rhythm can also permanently fix positive thoughts in our minds. Are you currently aware of any positive thoughts that have firmly been repeated in your mind? If so, list them.

16. To delve deeper into hypnotic rhythm, if your mind fears poverty, it will attract it. Similarly, if your mind demands opulence and expects it, it will attract the physical and financial equivalents of opulence. Take some time to list both the negative and positive messages that your mind plays out on an ongoing basis.

17. Now that you have your list, as your "other self," share any additional thought patterns you have that you may not be consciously aware of. List them.

Study Guide   137

18. Did you understand the Bible quote, "Whatsoever a man soweth, that shall he also reap," to reflect the law of attraction? Please explain.

19. We are where we are not only in response to our deeds, but also in response to our thoughts. Do you believe your thoughts vastly impact your life? Do you have evidence of how they do or do not affect your life? Please list them.

20. According to the Devil, "luck" and "miracles" are twin sisters that are misunderstood. The root of these happenings can be too far removed to explain; thus, they are deemed as such. Do you believe in luck or miracles? Do you believe they could be rooted in cause and effect, and not random?

21. Napoleon Hill asks the Devil where he dwells and operates other than in the minds of people. He lists many of the places he resides. For each, state whether you have experienced him in that place:
    - The explosion in lightning. (yes/no)
    - The pain in disease and physical suffering. (yes/no)
    - The unseen general in warfare. (yes/no)
    - The unknown commissioner of poverty and famine. (yes/no)
    - The executioner extraordinaire at death. (yes/no)
    - The inspirer of lust after flesh. (yes/no)
    - The creator of jealousy, envy, and greed. (yes/no)
    - The instigator of fear. (yes/no)
    - The genius who converts the achievements of men of science into instruments of death. (yes/no)
    - The destroyer of harmony in all manner of human relationships. (yes/no)
    - The destroyer of harmony in all manner of human relationships. (yes/no)
    - The antithesis of justice. (yes/no)
    - The driving force in all immorality. (yes/no)
    - The statement of all good. (yes/no)
    - Anxiety, suspense, superstition, and insanity. (yes/no)
    - The destroyer of hope and faith. (yes/no)
    - The inspirer of destructive gossip and scandal. (yes/no)
    - The discourager of free and independent thought. (yes/no)
    - The creator of all forms of human misery. (yes/no)
    - The instigator of discouragement and disappointment. (yes/no)

22. The Devil asserts that nondrifters "do not wait for opportunity to be placed in their way. They create opportunity to fit their desires and demands of life!" How have you "created" opportunities in your life?

23. At the end of this chapter Napoleon Hill asks why the opposition does not use hypnotic rhythm more potently to outwit the Devil with the placement of more positive thoughts into the mind of humankind. The Devil asserts that he makes negative thinking and destructive deeds pleasing to man and that his bribes are more attractive because of this. What are your thoughts on this? Do you believe that negative thinking in general is more attractive to humankind than positive? Please explain.

Chapter 7

Seeds of Fear

Q I have often wondered why your opposition—what we earthbound call God—does not annihilate you? Can you tell me why?
A. Because the power is as much mine as his. It is as available to me as to him. That is what I have been trying to get over to you. The highest power in the universe can be used for constructive purposes, through what you call God, or it can be used for negative purposes, through what you call the Devil. And something more important still, it can be used by any human being just as effectively as by God or the Devil.

Q You make a far-reaching claim. Can you prove your claim?
A. Yes, but it would be better if you proved it for yourself. The Devil's word is not worth much among you earthbound sinners. Neither is God's word. You fear the Devil and refuse to trust your God; therefore you have but one source available through which you may appropriate the benefit of universal power, and that is by trusting and using your own power of thought. This is the direct road to the universal storehouse of Infinite Intelligence. There is no other road available to any human being.

Q. Why have we earthbound not found the road to Infinite Intelligence sooner?

A. Because I have intercepted you and led you off the path by planting in your minds thoughts which destroy your power to use your minds constructively. I have made it attractive to you to use the Power of Infinite Intelligence to attain negative ends, through greed, avarice, lust, envy, and hatred. Remember, your mind attracts that which your mind dwells upon. To divert you away from my opposition, I had only to feed you on thoughts helpful to my cause.

Q. If I understand what you are saying, you are admitting that no human being need fear the Devil or worry about how to flatter God!

A. That is it precisely. This admission may put a crimp in my style, but I have this satisfaction of knowing it may also slow down my opposition by sending people direct to the source of all power.

Q. In other words, if you cannot control people through negative bribes or fear, then you wish to kick over the entire apple cart and show people how to go directly to God? Are you, by any chance, in politics too? Your technique seems frightfully familiar.

A. Am I in politics? If I am not in politics, who do you believe starts depressions and forces people into wars? Surely you would not lay this at the door of my opposition. As I have already told you, I have allies in all walks of life, to help me in connection with all human relationships.

Q. Why don't you take over the churches and use them outright in your cause?

A. Do you think I am a fool? Who would keep alive the fear of the Devil if I subdued the churches? Who would serve as a decoy to attract the attention of people while I manipulate their minds if I did not have some agency through which to sow the seeds of fear and doubt? The cleverest thing I do is to use the allies of my opposition to keep the fear of hell burning in the minds of people. As long as people fear something, no matter what, I will keep a grip on them.

Q. I am beginning to see your scheme. You use the churches to plant the seed of fear and uncertainty and indefiniteness in the minds of people. These negative states of mind cause people to form the habit of drifting. This habit crystallizes into permanency through the law of hypnotic rhythm; then the victim is helpless to help himself, is that right? Hypnotic rhythm, then, is something to be watched and respected?

A. A better way of stating the truth is that hypnotic rhythm is something to be studied, understood, and voluntarily applied to attain definite desired ends.

Q. If the force of hypnotic rhythm is not voluntarily applied to attain definite ends, may it be a great danger?

A. Yes, and for the reason that it operates automatically. If it is not consciously applied to attain a desired end, it can, and it will, operate to attain undesired ends.

Take the simple illustration of climate, for example. Anyone can see and understand that nature forces every living thing and every element of matter to adjust itself to her climates. In the tropics she creates trees which bear fruit and reproduce themselves. She forces the trees to adjust themselves to her scorching sun! She forces them to put out leaves suitable for protection against the rays of the sun. These same trees could not survive if removed to the arctic regions where nature has established an entirely different climate.

In the colder climate she creates trees which are adjusted to survive and to reproduce themselves, but they could not survive if transplanted in the tropical regions. In the same manner, nature clothes her animals, giving to those in each different climate a covering suited to their comfort and survival in that climate.

In a similar manner, nature forces upon the minds of men the influences of their environment, which are stronger than the individual's own thoughts. Children are forced to take on the nature of all influences of those around them unless their own thoughts are stronger than the influences.

Nature sets up a definite rhythm for every environment, and everything within the range of that rhythm is forced to conform to it. Man, alone, has the power to establish his own rhythm of thought providing he exercises this privilege before hypnotic rhythm has forced upon him the influences of his environment.

Every home, every place of business, every town and village and every street and community center has its own definite, discernible rhythm. If you wish to know what a difference there is in the rhythms of streets, take a walk up Fifth Avenue, in New York, and then down a street in the slums! All forms of rhythm become permanent with time.

Q Does each individual have his own rhythm of thought?
A. Yes. That is precisely the major difference between individuals. The person who thinks in terms of power, success, opulence, sets up a rhythm which attracts these desirable possessions. The person who thinks in terms of misery, failure, defeat, discouragement, and poverty attracts these undesirable influences. This explains why both success and failure are the result of habit. Habit establishes one's rhythm of thought, and that rhythm attracts the object of one's dominating thoughts.

Q Hypnotic rhythm is something resembling a magnet which attracts things for which it has a magnetic affinity. Is that correct?
A. Yes, that is correct. That is why the poverty-stricken herd themselves into the same communities. It explains that old saying, "Misery loves company." It also explains why people who begin to

succeed in any undertaking find that success multiplies, with less effort, as time goes on.

All successful people use hypnotic rhythm, either consciously or unconsciously, by expecting and demanding success. The demand becomes a habit, hypnotic rhythm takes over the habit, and the law of harmonious attraction translates it into its physical equivalent.

Q. In other words, if I know what I want from life, demand it and back my demand by a willingness to pay life's price for what I want, and refuse to accept any substitutes, the law of hypnotic rhythm takes over my desire and helps, by natural and logical means, to transmute it into its physical counterpart. Is that true?

A. That describes the way the law works.

Q. Science has established irrefutable evidence that people are what they are because of heredity and environment. They bring over with them at birth a combination of all the physical qualities of all their numberless ancestors. After they arrive here, they reach the age of self-consciousness and from there on they shape their own personalities and more or less fix their own earthly destinations as the result of the environmental influences to which they are subjected, especially the influences which control them during early childhood. These two facts have been so well established there is no room for any intelligent person to question them. How can hypnotic rhythm change the nature of a physical body which is a combination of thousands of ancestors who have lived and died before one is born? How can hypnotic rhythm change the influence of one's environment? People who are born in poverty and ignorance have a strong tendency to remain poverty-stricken and ignorant all through life. What, if anything, can hypnotic rhythm do about this?

A. Hypnotic rhythm cannot change the nature of the physical body one inherits at birth, but it can and it does modify, change, control, and make permanent one's environmental influences.

Q If I understand what you mean, a human being is forced by nature to take on and become a part of the environment he chooses or the environment that may be forced upon him?

A. That is correct, but there are ways and means by which an individual may resist the influences of an environment he does not wish to accept, and also a method of procedure by which one may reverse the application of hypnotic rhythm from negative to positive ends.

Q Do you mean that there is a definite method by which hypnotic rhythm can be made to serve instead of destroy one?

A. I mean just that.

Q Tell me how this astounding end may be attained.

A. For my description to be of any practical value, it will be necessarily lengthy because it will have to cover seven principles of psychology which must be understood and applied by all who use hypnotic rhythm to aid them in forcing life to yield that which they want.

Q Then break your description into seven parts, each giving a detailed analysis of one of the seven principles, with simple instructions for its practical application.

STUDY GUIDE

Chapter 7:
Seeds of Fear

1. The Devil opens this chapter sharing that he and his "opposition" (that is, God, Universal Creator) both have equal power that can be used for whatever we want. The choice is ours. What do you believe has been at the root of your life choices to date—fear or love? Please explain.

2. According to the Devil, due to humankind's fear of the Devil and distrust of God, the way to prove their existence is through your own power of thought. On a scale of 1 to 10 (1 being "very little" and 10 being "very much so"), rate the degree to which you are interested in experiencing and exploring the universal storehouse of Infinite Intelligence:
1 — 2 — 3 — 4 — 5 — 6 — 7 — 8 — 9 — 10

3. It is confirmed that no human need to fear the Devil nor flatter God. Do you believe this to be true? Why or why not?

4. Do you see evidence of this belief? Please explain.

5. The Devil states that he uses fear that is planted in the minds of people through politics, the churches, and any other institutions that perpetuate his power and instill fear of him. While you honor your religious experience, could this vice be possible? Why or why not?

6. Reflect on your response to the previous question. Could your response be based on any fearful thoughts? Fear of retribution for questioning? Fear of punishment for not following those beliefs with which you have been raised? Please explain.

7. It is stated that if hypnotic rhythm is not applied consciously and voluntarily to "attain a desired end, then it can, and it will, operate to attain undesired end." List some examples of this in the world today.

8. Nature is used as an example of how it forces every living thing and every element of matter to adjust itself to her climates. If this were the case, nature will adjust to the climate changes that we fear are pending. Taking this a step further, if nature can adjust, is the issue more than humankind can address? Please share your thoughts on this topic.

9. According to the Devil, every business, home, village, town, city, street, and community center has its own discernible rhythm. Reflect on your current environment. How would you describe the rhythm of the following: your home, your business, your street, your place of worship, your community center, your local shopping plaza, your street, your favorite restaurant, and your favorite coffee shop?

10. It is further stated that we each have our own rhythm, which is reflected in the experiences we are having in our lives. Reflect on your current experiences. Are they mainly based in "power, success and opulence" or in "misery, failure, defeat, discouragement and poverty"?

11. Are you happy with your current rhythm, or would you like to change it?

12. What habits do you possess, or have you possessed, that have led you to your current state? Please explain.

13. Where do you see evidence of "misery loves company" in the world? Do you see it in your local world?

14. How have you seen the "law of harmonious attraction" exemplified in the world? Give at least one example.

15. While hypnotic rhythm cannot change the nature of the physical body, according to the Devil, it can change one's environment. Do you believe this to be so? Why or why not? Share examples to substantiate your belief.

Chapter 8

Definiteness of Purpose

Q Your Majesty will now proceed to unfold the secrets of the seven principles through which human beings may force life to provide them with spiritual, mental, and physical freedom.

Do not be sparing in your description of these principles. I want a complete illustration of how the principles may be used by anyone who chooses to use them. Tell us all you know about the principle of *definiteness of purpose.*

A. If you go through with this mad idea of publishing my confession, you will open the gates of hell and turn loose all the precious souls I have collected back down through the ages. You will deprive me of souls yet unborn. You will release from my bondage millions now living. Stop, I beg of you.

Q Open up. Let's hear what you have to say about the principle of definiteness of purpose.

A. You are pouring water on the fires of hell, but the responsibility is yours, not mine. I may as well tell you that any human being who can be definite in his aims and plans can make life hand over whatever is wanted.

Q That is a broad claim, Your Majesty. Do you wish to tone it down a bit?

A. Tone it down? No, I wish to tone it up. When you hear what I now have to say, you will understand why the principle of definiteness is so important. My opposition uses a clever little trick to cheat me of my control over people. The opposition knows that definiteness of purpose closes the door of one's mind so tightly against me that I cannot break through unless I can induce one to form the habit of drifting.

Q Why doesn't your opposition give your secret to all people by telling them to avoid you through definiteness of purpose? You have already admitted that two out of every hundred people belong to your opposition.

A. Because I am more clever than my opposition. I draw people away from definiteness with my promises. You see, I control more people than my opposition because I am a better salesman and a better showman. I attract people by feeding them liberally of the thought-habits in which they like to indulge.

Q Is definiteness of purpose something with which one must be born or may it be acquired?

A. Everyone, as I have told you before, is born with the privilege of being definite, but 98 out of every 100 people lose this privilege by sleeping on it. The privilege of definiteness can be maintained only by adopting it as a policy by which one is guided in all the affairs of life.

Q Oh, I see! One takes advantage of the principle of definiteness just as one may build a strong physical body—through constant, systematic use. Is that it?

A. You have stated the truth clearly and accurately.

Q Now I think we are getting somewhere, Your Majesty. We have at long last found the starting point from which all who become self-determining in life must take off.

We have discovered, from your astounding confession, that your greatest asset is man's lack of caution, which enables you to lead him into the jungle of indefiniteness through simple bribes.

We have learned, beyond the question of doubt, that anyone who adopts definiteness of purpose as a policy and uses it in all of his daily experiences cannot be induced to form the habit of drifting. Without the aid of the drifting habit you are powerless to attract people through promises. Is this correct?

A. I couldn't have stated the truth more clearly myself.

Q Go ahead, now, and describe how people neglect their privilege of being free and self-determining through indefiniteness and drifting.

A. I have already made brief reference to this principle, but I will now go into more minute details as to how the principle works.

I shall have to begin at the time of birth. When a child is born, it brings with it nothing but a physical body representing the evolutionary results of millions of years of ancestry.

Its mind is a total blank. When the child reaches the age of consciousness and begins to recognize the objects of its surroundings, it begins, also, to imitate others.

Imitation becomes a fixed habit. Naturally the child imitates, first of all, its parents! Then it begins to imitate its other relatives and daily associates, including its religious instructors and schoolteachers.

The imitation extends not merely to physical expression, but also to thought expression. If a child's parents fear me and express that fear within range of the child's hearing, the child picks up the fear through the habit of imitation and stores it away as a part of its subconscious stock of beliefs.

If the child's religious instructor expresses any form of fear of me (and they all do, in one form or another), that fear is added to the similar fear passed to the child by its parents, and the two forms of negative limitation are stored away in the subconscious mind to be drawn upon and used by me later in life.

In a similar way the child learns, by imitation, to limit its power of thought by filling its mind with envy, hatred, greed, lust, revenge, and all the other negative impulses of thought which destroy all possibility of definiteness.

Meanwhile I move in and induce the child to drift until I bind its mind through hypnotic rhythm.

Q Am I to understand from your remarks that you have to gain control of people while they are very young or lose your opportunity at them altogether?

A. I prefer to claim them before they come into possession of their own minds. Once any person learns the power of his own thoughts, he becomes positive and difficult to subdue. As a matter of fact, I cannot control any human being who discovers and uses the principle of definiteness.

Q Is the habit of definiteness a permanent protection against your control?

A. No, not by any means. Definiteness closes the door of one's mind to me only as long as that person follows the principle as a matter of policy. Once any person hesitates, procrastinates, or becomes indefinite about anything, he is just one step removed from my control.

Q What has definiteness to do with one's material circumstances? I want to know if one may acquire power through definiteness of purpose without inviting destruction through the law of compensation.

A. Your question limits my illustrations because there are so few people in the world who understand, and there have been so few in the past who understood, how to use definiteness of purpose without attracting to themselves the negative application of the law of compensation.

Here you are forcing me to disclose one of my most prized tricks. I am bound to tell you that I eventually reclaim for my cause all who escape me temporarily through definiteness of purpose. The reclamation is made by filling the mind with greed for power and the love of egotistical expression, until the individual falls into the habit of violating the rights of others. Then I step in with the law of compensation and reclaim my victim.

Q So I see from your admission that definiteness of purpose may be dangerous in proportion to its possibility as a power. Is that true?

A. Yes, and what is more important, every principle of good carries with it the seed of an equivalent danger.

Q That is hard to believe. What danger, for example, can there be in the habit of love of truth?

A. The danger lies in the word "habit." All habits, save only that of the love of definiteness of purpose, may lead to the habit of drifting. Love for truth, unless it assumes the proportion of definite pursuit of truth, may become similar to all other good intentions. You know, of course, what I do with good intentions.

Q Is love for one's relatives also dangerous?

A. The love for anything or anyone, save only the love of definiteness of purpose, may become dangerous. Love is a state of mind which beclouds reason, saps will power, and blinds one to facts and truth.

Everyone who becomes self-determining and gains spiritual freedom to think his own thoughts must examine carefully every emotion that seems even remotely related to love.

You may be surprised to know that love is one of my most effective baits. With it I lead into the habit of drifting those whom I could attract with nothing else.

That is why I have placed it at the head of my list of bribes. Show me what any person loves most and I will have my cue as to how that person can be induced to drift until I bind him with hypnotic rhythm.

Love and fear, combined, give me the most effective weapons with which I induce people to drift. One is as helpful to me as the other. Both have the effect of causing people to neglect to develop definiteness in the use of their own minds. Give me control over a person's fears and tell me what he loves most and you may as well mark that person down as my slave. Both love and fear are emotional forces of such stupendous potency that either may completely set aside the power of will and the power of reason. Without will and reason there is nothing left to support definiteness of purpose.

Q But, Your Majesty, life would not be worth living if people never felt the emotion of love.

A. Ah! You are right as far as your reasoning goes, but you neglected to add that love should be under one's definite control at all times.

Of course, love is a desirable state of mind, but it also is a palliative which may be used to limit or destroy reason and will power, both of which rate above love in importance to human beings who want freedom and self-determination.

Q I understand from what you say that people who gain power must harden their emotions, master fear, and subdue love. Is that correct?

A. People who gain and maintain power must become definite in all their thoughts and all their deeds. If that is what you call hard, then they must become hard.

Q Let us look into the sources of advantage of definiteness in the everyday affairs of life. Which is more apt to succeed, a weak plan applied with definiteness, or a sound strong plan indefinitely applied?

A. Weak plans have a way of becoming strong if definitely applied.

Q You mean that any plan definitely put into continuous action in pursuit of a definite purpose may be successful even if it is not the best plan?

A. Yes, I mean just that. Definiteness of purpose plus definiteness of plan by which the purpose is to be achieved generally succeeds, no matter how weak the plan may be. The major difference between a sound and an unsound plan is that the sound plan, if definitely applied, may be carried out more quickly than an unsound plan.

Q In other words, if one cannot be always right one can and should be always definite? Is that what you are trying to get across to me?

A. That is the idea. People who are definite in both their plans and their purposes never accept temporary defeat as being more than an urge to greater effort. You can see for yourself that this sort of policy is bound to win if it is followed with definiteness.

Q Can a person who moves with definiteness of both plan and purpose be always sure of success?

A. No. The best of plans sometimes misfire, but the person who moves with definiteness recognizes the difference between temporary defeat and failure. When plans fail he substitutes others but he does not change his purpose. He perseveres. Eventually he finds a plan that succeeds.

Q Will a plan based upon immoral or unjust ends succeed as quickly as one motivated by a keen sense of justice and morality?

A. Through the operation of the law of compensation, everyone reaps that which he sows. Plans based on unjust or immoral motives may bring temporary success, but enduring success must take into consideration the fourth dimension, time.

Time is the enemy of immorality and injustice. It is the friend of justice and morality. Failure to recognize this fact has been responsible for the crime wave among the youths of the world.

The youthful, inexperienced mind is apt to mistake temporary success for permanency. The youth often makes the mistake of coveting the temporary gains of immoral, unjust plans, but neglects to look ahead and observe the penalties which follow as definitely as night follows day.

STUDY GUIDE

Chapter 8:
Definiteness of Purpose

1. The seven principles of definite purpose are said to provide you with spiritual, mental, and physical freedom. On a scale of 1 to 10 (1 being "very little" and 10 being "very much so"), rate the degree to which you feel free in each area of your life:

   Spiritually Free:
   1 — 2 — 3 — 4 — 5 — 6 — 7 — 8 — 9 — 10

   Mentally Free:
   1 — 2 — 3 — 4 — 5 — 6 — 7 — 8 — 9 — 10

   Physically Free:
   1 — 2 — 3 — 4 — 5 — 6 — 7 — 8 — 9 — 10

2. In this discourse, Napoleon Hill wrote that by publishing his confession, the Devil will "open the gates of hell and turn loose all the precious souls I have collected back down through the ages" and "deprive me of souls yet unborn." Do you believe this to be possible? Why or why not? Please explain.

3. The Devil states that "any human being who can be definite in his aims and plans can make life hand over whatever is wanted." Write a list of all those things, experiences, or shifts that you want in your life, but have not yet manifested.

4. The Devil claims to be cleverer, a better salesman than his opposition. Do you believe this to be possible? Why or why not?

5. While all are born with the privilege of being definite, just like exercise is required to build a strong physical body, definiteness of purpose must also be constantly and systematically used. On a scale of 1 to

10 (1 being "very little" and 10 being "very much so"), rate the degree to which you feel you are disciplined:

1 —— 2 —— 3 —— 4 —— 5 —— 6 —— 7 —— 8 —— 9 —— 10

6. The Devil describes the ways in which people neglect their privilege of being free and self-determining through indefiniteness of purpose. Take some time and reflect on what you wish to manifest now in your life. Is there anything in response to which you are not definite? If so, either take it off your list or take the steps you need to become more definite.

7. It is said that children imitate their parents, teachers, and others in their lives. They can sense the fear that is expressed within their range of hearing. Do you ever remember hearing your parents or family members expressing fear? If so, do you believe that you were affected by their fear?

8. Did you receive religious instruction that expressed some form of fear as a child? If so, what effect do you believe it had on you?

9. Children also learn envy, hatred, greed, lust, revenge, and all other negative impulses through those in their environment, especially from parents, teachers, and clergy. Reflect on your childhood as to when you first started feeling each of these negative emotions. Do you feel you picked up some feelings from those around you? Please explain.

10. Through hesitation, procrastination, or indefiniteness you can become vulnerable to drifting. When do you find yourself tending to drift. Can you note a pattern? For example, do you procrastinate before beginning a project, or just before breaking through?

11. The Devil reclaims his cause through filling the mind with "greed for power and the love of egotistical expression." When one violates the rights of others, he then steps in with the law of compensation and reclaims his victims. Have you seen this play out in your life or in the life of your loved ones? If so, how?

12. The Devil states that for every positive purpose, a negative one can potentially develop, even in the case of love. He states that love can cloud reason, sap willpower, and blind one to facts and truth. Can you give an example of how this can happen, especially in your life?

13. The Devil states, "Give me control over a person's fears and tell me what he loves most, and you may as well mark that person down as my slave." Because love and fear are such potent emotions, willpower

and reason can easily be set aside. Consider a time when you were overwhelmed with fear in your life. Could you have lost willpower and reason under the circumstances you were in? Please explain.

14. Napoleon Hill asks the Devil to confirm that people who gain power must "harden their emotions, master fear, and subdue love." This sounds harsh. Do you believe this to be so? Why or why not?

15. It is further stated that "any plan definitely put into continuous action in pursuit of a definite purpose may be successful even if it is not the best plan." While sound plans can be carried out more quickly, any plan followed with a definiteness of purpose will succeed. Reflect on your life. Can you think of a plan that you had where there was complete definiteness of purpose that you completed quickly and successfully? Similarly, did you ever have a plan that was not as good a plan that, while it took longer, was still a success? Please describe it.

16. It is said that you should accept temporary defeat as no more than an "urge to greater effort." Focus on one area in which you recently felt defeated in your life. Did you view it as only a temporary defeat? If not, can you shift your perspective?

17. The Devil goes on to assert "that which we reap, we sow." Do you believe this to be true? If so, write about one such situation in your life, both where negativity reaped further negativity and positivity reaped further positivity.

18. The Devil states that "time is the enemy of immorality and injustice and the friend to justice and morality." He cites the youth as misperceiving temporary success as permanent, failing to observe the penalties that follow. Do you believe this to be true? If so, what evidence do you see of this in the world?

Chapter 9

Education and Religion

Q This is pretty deep stuff, Your Majesty. Let us get back to the discussion of lighter and more concrete subjects that are likely to interest the majority of people. I am interested in discussing the things that make people happy and miserable, rich and poor, sick and healthy. In brief, I am interested in everything that can be used by human beings to make life pay satisfactory dividends in return for the effort that one puts into the business of living.

A. Very well, let us be definite.

Q You have my idea. Your Majesty has a tendency to stray off into abstract details which most people can neither understand nor use in the solution of their problems. Could that, by any chance, be a definite plan of yours to answer my questions with indefinite answers? If that is your plan, it is a slick trick but it will not work. Go ahead now and tell me something more of the miseries and failures of human beings growing directly out of indefiniteness.

A. Why not permit me to tell you more of the pleasures and successes of people who understand and apply the principle of definiteness?

Q I observe that sometimes people with definiteness of plan and purpose get what they ask from life only to find after they get it that they do not want it. What then?

A. Generally one can get rid of whatever is not wanted by application of the same principle of definiteness with which the thing was acquired. A life that is lived with fullness of peace of mind, contentment, and happiness always divests itself of everything it does not want. Anyone who submits to annoyance by things he does not want is not definite. He is a drifter.

Q What about married people who cease to want each other? Should they separate, or is it true that all marriages are made in heaven and the contracting parties are, therefore, forever bound by their bargain, even though it may prove to be a poor one for both.

A. First, let me correct that old saying that all marriages are made in heaven. I know of some which were made on my side of the fence. Minds which do not harmonize should never be forced to remain together in marriage or any other relationship. Friction and all forms of discord between minds lead inevitably to the habit of drifting, and of course to indefiniteness.

Q Aren't people sometimes bound to others by a relationship of duty which renders it impractical for them to take from life what they want most?

A. "Duty" is one of the most abused and misunderstood words in existence. The first duty of every human being is to himself. Every person owes himself the duty of finding how to live a full and happy life. Beyond this, if one has time and energy not needed in the fulfillment of his own desires, one may assume responsibility for helping others.

Q Isn't that a selfish attitude, and isn't selfishness one of the causes of failure to find happiness?

A. I stand by my statement that there is no higher duty than that which one owes himself.

Q Doesn't a child owe something in the way of duty to its parents who gave it life and sustenance during its periods of helplessness?

A. Not at all. It is just the other way around. Parents owe their children everything they can give them in the way of knowledge. Beyond that, parents often spoil instead of helping their offspring by a false sense of duty which prompts them to indulge their children instead of forcing them to seek and gain knowledge at first hand.

Q I see what you mean. Your theory is that too much help thrust upon the youth encourages him to drift and become indefinite in all things. You believe that necessity is a teacher of great sagacity, that defeat carries with it an equivalent virtue, that unearned gifts of every nature may become a curse instead of a blessing. Is that correct?

A. You have stated my philosophy perfectly. My belief is not theory. It is fact.

Q Then you do not advocate prayer as a means of gaining desirable ends?

A. On the contrary I do advocate prayer, but not the sort of prayer that consists of empty, begging, meaningless words.

The sort of prayer against which I am helpless is the prayer of definiteness of purpose.

Q I never thought of definiteness of purpose as being a prayer. How can it be?

A. Definiteness is in effect the only sort of prayer upon which one can rely. It places one in the way of using hypnotic rhythm to attain definite ends ... by the mere act of appropriating it from the great universal storehouse of Infinite Intelligence. The appropriation, in case you are interested, takes place through definiteness of purpose, persistently pursued!

Q. Why do the majority of prayers fail?
A. They don't. All prayers bring that for which one prays.

Q. But you just said that definiteness of purpose is the only sort of prayer upon which one can rely. Now you say that all prayers bring results. What do you mean?
A. There is nothing inconsistent about it. The majority of people who pray go to prayer only after everything else fails them. Naturally they go with their minds filled with fear that the prayers will not be answered. Well, their fears are realized.

The person who goes to prayer with definiteness of purpose and faith in the attainment of that purpose puts into motion the laws of nature which transmute one's dominating desires into their physical equivalent. That is all there is to prayer.

One form of prayer is negative and brings only negative results. One form is positive and brings definite, positive results. Could anything be more simple?

People who whine and beg God to assume responsibility for all their troubles and provide them with all the necessities and luxuries of life are too lazy to create what they want and translate it into existence through the power of their own minds.

When you hear a person praying for something that he should procure through his own efforts, you may be sure you are listening to a drifter.

Infinite Intelligence favors only those who understand and adapt themselves to her laws. She makes no discrimination because of fine character or pleasing personality. These things help people negotiate their way through life more harmoniously with one another, but the source from which prayer is answered is not impressed by fine feathers. Nature's law is, "Know what you want, adapt yourself to my laws, and you shall have it."

Q Does that harmonize with the teachings of Christ?

A. Perfectly. Also it harmonizes with the teachings of all truly great philosophers.

Q Is your theory of definiteness in harmony with the philosophy of men of science?

A. Definiteness is the major difference between a scientist and a drifter. Through the principle of definiteness of purpose and plan, the scientist forces nature to hand over her most profound secrets. It was through this principle that Edison uncovered the secret of the talking machine, the incandescent electric light, and scores of other benefits for mankind.

Q Then I understand that definiteness is the first requisite for success in all earthly undertakings? Is that right?

A. Exactly! Anything which teaches people to examine facts and coordinate them into definite plans through accurate thinking is hard on my profession. If this thirst for definite knowledge now spreading over the world keeps up, my business will be shot to pieces within the next few centuries. I thrive on ignorance, superstition, intolerance, and fear, but I cannot stand up under definite knowledge properly organized into definite plans in the minds of people who think for themselves.

Q Why don't you take over Omnipotence and manage the whole works in your own way?

A. You might as well ask why the negative portion of the electron doesn't take over the positive portion and run the entire works. The answer is that both the positive and the negative charges of energy are necessary to the existence of the electron. One is balanced equally against the other, stalemated, as it were.

So it is with what you call Omnipotence and I. We represent the positive and the negative forces of the entire system of universes, and we are equally balanced one against the other.

If this power of balance were shifted the slightest degree, the whole system of universes would become quickly reduced to a mass of inert matter. Now you know why I cannot take over the whole show and run it my way.

Q. If what you say is true, you have exactly the same power as Omnipotence. Is that true?
A. That is correct. My opposition—you call it Omnipotence—expresses itself through the forces which you call good, the positive forces of nature. I express myself through the forces you call bad, the negative forces. Both good and bad are coincidental with existence. One is as important as the other.

Q. Then the doctrine of predestination is sound. People are born to success or failure, misery or happiness, to be good or bad, and they have nothing to do with this nor can they modify their natures. Is that your claim?
A. Emphatically not! Every human being has a wide range of choice in both his thoughts and his deeds. Every human being can use his brain for the reception and the expression of positive thoughts or he can use it for the expression of negative thoughts. His choice in this important matter shapes his entire life.

Q. From what you have said I gather the idea that human beings have more freedom of expression than either you or your opposition. Is that correct?
A. That is true. Omnipotence and I are bound by immutable laws of nature. We cannot express ourselves in any manner not conforming to these laws.

Q. Then it is true that man has rights and privileges not available to either Omnipotence or the Devil. Is that the truth?
A. Yes, that is true, but you might well have added that man has not yet fully awakened to the realization of this potential power.

Man still regards himself as something resembling the worms in the dust, when in reality he has more power than all other living things combined.

Q. Definiteness of purpose seems to be a panacea for all evils of man.

A. Not that perhaps, but you may be sure no one ever will become self-determining without it.

Q. Why aren't children taught definiteness of purpose in the public schools?

A. For the reason that there is no definite plan or purpose behind any of the school curricula! Children are sent to school to make credits and to learn how to memorize, not to learn what they want of life.

Q. What good is a school credit if one cannot convert it into the material and spiritual needs of life?

A. I am only a Devil, not an unwinder of riddles!

Q. I deduce from all you say that neither the schools nor the churches prepare the youths of the world with a practical working knowledge of their own minds. Is anything of more importance to a human being than an understanding of the forces and circumstances which influence his own mind?

A. The only thing of enduring value to any human being is a working knowledge of his own mind. The churches do not permit a person to inquire into the possibilities of his own mind, and the schools do not recognize that such a thing as a mind exists.

Q. Aren't you a little hard on the schools and the churches?

A. No, I am merely describing them as they are, without bias or prejudice.

Q Aren't the schools and the churches your bitter enemies?
A. Their leaders may think they are, but I am impressed only by facts. The truth is this, if you must know it: the churches are my most helpful allies and the schools run the churches a close second.

Q On what specific or general grounds do you make this claim?
A. On the grounds that both the churches and the schools help me to convert people to the habit of drifting.

Q Do you realize that your charge is substantially a sweeping indictment of the two institutions of major importance which have been responsible for civilization, in its present form?
A. Do I realize it? Man alive, I gloat over it. If the schools and churches had taught people how to think for themselves, where would I be, now?

Q This confession of yours will disillusion millions of people whose only hope for salvation is in their churches. Isn't that a cruel thing to do to them?
Wouldn't most people be better off living in the bliss of ignorance than to know the truth about you?
A. What do you mean by the term "salvation"? From what are people being saved? The only form of enduring salvation that is worth a green fig to any human being is that which comes from recognition of the power of his own mind. Ignorance and fear are the only enemies from which men need salvation.

Q You seem to hold nothing sacred.
A. You are wrong. I hold sacred the one thing which is my master—the one thing I fear.

Q What is that?
A. The power of independent thought backed by definiteness of purpose.

Q Then you do not have many people to fear?
A. Only two out of every 100 to be exact. I control all others.

Q Let's give the churches a rest and get back to the public schools. Your confession has shown clearly that you thrive and perpetuate yourself from one generation to another by the clever trick of taking over the minds of children before they have the chance to learn how to use their minds.

I wish to know what is wrong with a public school system that permits the Devil to control so many people. I wish to know, also, what can be done to the established system of teaching that will insure all children the opportunity to learn, first, that they have minds, and second, how to use those minds to bring spiritual and economic freedom.

I am putting the question to you definitely enough, and since you have stressed the importance of definiteness of purpose I am here and now putting you on notice that your answer to my question must be definite.

A. Wait a moment while I catch my breath. You have given me quite an order! It seems strange that you would come to the Devil to learn how to live. I should think you would go to my opposition. Why don't you?

Q Your Majesty, it is you who are on trial here, not I. I want the truth and I am not particular as to the source from which I get it. There is something radically wrong with the system of education that has given us a balance sheet with life that shows us hopelessly in the red and groping for the road to self-determination as if we were so many animals lost in the jungle.

I want to know two things about this system. First, what is the major weakness of the system? Second, how can this weakness be eliminated? The floor is yours again! Please stick to the question and stop trying to decoy me into the discussion of deep, abstract subjects. That's definite, is it not?

A. You leave me no choice but that of direct answer. To begin with, the public school system approaches the subject of education from the wrong angle. The school system endeavors to teach children to memorize facts, instead of teaching them how to use their own minds.

Q Is that all that is wrong with the system?
A. No, that is only the beginning. Another major weakness of the school system is that it does not establish in the minds of children either the importance of definiteness of purpose or make any attempt to teach youths how to be definite about anything.

The major object of all schooling is to force the students to cram their memories with facts instead of teaching them how to organize and make practical use of facts.

This cramming system centers the attention of students on the accumulation of "credits" but overlooks the important question of how to use knowledge in the practical affairs of life. This system turns out graduates whose names are inscribed upon parchment certificates, but whose minds are empty of self-determination. The school system got off to a bad start at the beginning. The schools began as institutions of "higher learning," operated entirely for the select few whose wealth and family entitled them to education.

Thus the entire school system was evolved by beginning at the top and working back down to the bottom. It is no wonder the system neglects to teach children the importance of definiteness of purpose when the system, itself, has literally evolved through indefiniteness.

Q What would correct this weakness of the public school system? Let's not complain of the weakness of the system unless we are prepared to offer a practical remedy with which it can be corrected. In other words, while we are discussing the importance of definiteness of plan and purpose, let us take our own medicine and be definite.

A. Why don't you lay off the schools and churches and save yourself plenty of trouble? Don't you know that you are poking your nose into the affairs of the two forces that control the world? Suppose you do show up the schools and the churches as being weak and inadequate for the needs of human beings? What then? With what are you going to replace these two institutions?

Q. Stop trying to evade my questions by the old trick of asking a counter-question! I do not propose to replace the schools and churches. But I do propose to find out, if I can, how these organized forces can be modified so they will serve people instead of keeping them in ignorance. Go ahead, now, and give me a detailed catalogue of all the changes in the public school system which would improve it.

A. So you want the entire catalogue, do you? Do you want the suggested changes in the order of their importance?

Q. Describe the changes needed just as they come to you.

A. You are forcing me to commit an act of treason against myself, but here it is:

Reverse the present system by giving children the privilege of leading in their schoolwork instead of following orthodox rules designed only to impart abstract knowledge. Let instructors serve as students and let the students serve as instructors.

As far as possible, organize all schoolwork into definite methods through which the student can learn by doing, and direct the class work so that every student engages in some form of practical labor connected with the daily problems of life.

Ideas are the beginning of all human achievement. Teach all students how to recognize practical ideas that may be of benefit in helping them acquire whatever they demand of life.

Teach the students how to budget and use time, and above all teach the truth that time is the greatest asset available to human beings and the cheapest.

Teach the student the basic motives by which all people are influenced and show how to use these motives in acquiring the necessities and the luxuries of life.

Teach children what to eat, how much to eat, and what is the relationship between proper eating and sound health.

Teach children the true nature and function of the emotion of sex, and above all, teach them that it can be transmuted into a driving force capable of lifting one to great heights of achievement.

Teach children to be definite in all things, beginning with the choice of a definite major purpose in life!

Teach children the nature of and possibilities for good and evil in the principle of habit, using as illustrations with which to dramatize the subject the everyday experiences of children and adults.

Teach children how habits become fixed through the law of hypnotic rhythm, and influence them to adopt, while in the lower grades, habits that will lead to independent thought!

Teach children the difference between temporary defeat and failure, and show them how to search for the seed of an equivalent advantage which comes with every defeat.

Teach children to express their own thoughts fearlessly and to accept or reject, at will, all ideas of others, reserving to themselves, always, the privilege of relying upon their own judgment.

Teach children to reach decisions promptly and to change them, if at all, slowly and with reluctance, and never without a definite reason.

Teach children that the human brain is the instrument with which one receives, from the great storehouse of nature, the energy which is specialized into definite thoughts; that the brain does not think, but serves as an instrument for the interpretation of stimuli which cause thought.

Teach children the value of harmony in their own minds and that this is attainable only through self-control.

Teach children the nature and the value of self-control.

Teach children that there is a law of increasing returns which can be and should be put into operation, as a matter of habit, by rendering always more service and better service than is expected of them.

Teach children the true nature of the Golden Rule, and above all show them that through the operation of this principle, everything they do to and for another they do also to and for themselves.

Teach children not to have opinions unless they are formed from facts or beliefs which may reasonably be accepted as facts.

Teach children that cigarettes, liquor, narcotics, and overindulgence in sex destroy the power of will and lead to the habit of drifting. Do not forbid these evils—just explain them.

Teach children the danger of believing anything merely because their parents, religious instructors, or someone else says it is so.

Teach children to face facts, whether they are pleasant or unpleasant, without resorting to subterfuge or offering alibis.

Teach children to encourage the use of their sixth sense through which ideas present themselves in their minds from unknown sources, and to examine all such ideas carefully.

Teach children the full import of the law of compensation as it was interpreted by Ralph Waldo Emerson, and show them how the law works in the small, everyday affairs of life.

Teach children that definiteness of purpose, backed by definite plans persistently and continuously applied, is the most efficacious form of prayer available to human beings.

Teach children that the space they occupy in the world is measured definitely by the quality and quantity of useful service they render the world.

Teach children there is no problem which does not have an appropriate solution and that the solution often may be found in the circumstance creating the problem.

Teach children that their only real limitations are those which they set up or permit others to establish in their own minds.

Teach them that man can achieve whatever man can conceive and believe!

Teach children that all schoolhouses and all textbooks are elementary implements which may be helpful in the development of their minds, but that the only school of real value is the great University of Life wherein one has the privilege of learning from experience.

Teach children to be true to themselves at all times and, since they cannot please everybody, therefore to do a good job of pleasing themselves.

Q That is an imposing list, but it seems conspicuous by the fact it ignores practically every subject now taught in the public schools. Was that intended?
A. Yes. You asked for a list of suggested changes in public school curricula which would benefit children—well, that is what you got.

Q Some of the changes you suggest are so unorthodox they would shock most of the educators of today, wouldn't they?
A. Most of the educators of today need to be shocked. A good sound shock often helps the brain that has been atrophied by habit.

Q Would the changes you suggest for the public schools give children immunity against the habit of drifting?
A. Yes, that is one of the results the changes would bring, but there are others too.

Q How could the suggested changes be forced into the public school system? You know, of course, it is as difficult to get a new idea into an educator's brain as it is to interest a religious leader in modifying religion so it will help people to get more from life.

A. The quickest and surest way to force practical ideas into the public schools is to first introduce the ideas through private schools and establish such a demand for their use that public school officials will be compelled to employ them.

Q. Should any other changes be made in the public school system?
A. Yes, many. Among other changes needed in all public school programs is the addition of a complete course of training in the psychology of harmonious negotiation between people. All children should be taught how to sell their way through life with the minimum amount of friction.

Every public school should teach the principles of individual achievement through which one may attain a position of financial independence.

Classes should be abolished altogether. They should be replaced by the round table or conference system such as businessmen employ. All students should receive individual instruction and guidance in connection with subjects which cannot be properly taught in groups.

Every school should have an auxiliary group of instructors consisting of business and professional people, scientists, artists, engineers, and newspapermen, each of whom would impart to all the students a practical working knowledge of his own profession, business, or occupation. This instruction should be conducted through the conference system, to save the time of the instructors.

Q. What you have suggested is, in effect, an auxiliary system of instruction that would give all school children a working knowledge of the practical affairs of life, direct from the original source. Is that the idea?
A. You've stated it correctly.

Q. Let us dismiss the public school system and go back to the churches for a moment. All my life I have heard clergymen preaching against sin and warning sinners to beware and repent so they could be saved. But I have never heard any of them tell me what sin is. Will you give me some light on this subject?

A. Sin is anything one does or thinks which causes one to be unhappy! Human beings who are in sound physical and spiritual health should be at peace with themselves and always happy. Any form of mental or physical misery indicates the presence of sin.

Q. Name some of the common forms of sin.

A. It is a sin to overeat because that leads to ill health and misery.

It is a sin to over-indulge in sex because that breaks down one's will power and leads to the habit of drifting.

It is a sin to permit one's mind to be dominated by negative thoughts of envy, greed, fear, hatred, intolerance, vanity, self-pity, or discouragement, because these states of mind lead to the habit of drifting.

It is a sin to cheat, lie, and steal, because these habits destroy self-respect, subdue one's conscience, and lead to unhappiness.

It is a sin to remain in ignorance because that leads to poverty and loss of self-reliance.

It is a sin to accept from life anything one does not want because that indicates an unpardonable neglect to use the mind.

Q. Is it a sin for one to drift through life, without definite aim, plan, or purpose?

A. Yes, because this habit leads to poverty and destroys the privilege of self-determination. It also deprives one of the privilege of using his own mind as a medium of contact with Infinite Intelligence.

Q. Are you the chief inspirer of sin?

A. Yes! It is my business to gain control of the minds of people in every way possible.

Q Can you control the mind of a person who commits no sin?
A. I cannot, because that person never permits his mind to be dominated by any form of negative thought. I cannot enter the mind of one who never sins, let alone control it.

Q What is the commonest and most destructive of all sins?
A. Fear and ignorance.

Q Have you nothing else to add to the list?
A. There is nothing else to be added.

Q What is faith?
A. It is a state of mind wherein one recognizes and uses the power of positive thought as a medium by which one contacts and draws upon the universal store of Infinite Intelligence at will.

Q In other words, faith is the absence of all forms of negative thought. Is that the idea?
A. Yes, that is another way of describing it.

Q Has a drifter the capacity to use faith?
A. He may have the capacity but he does not use it. Everyone has the potential power to clear his mind of all negative thoughts and thereby avail himself of the power of faith.

Q Stating the matter in another way, faith is definiteness of purpose backed by belief in the attainment of the object of that purpose. Is that correct?
A. That's the idea, exactly.

STUDY GUIDE

Chapter 9:
Education and Religion

1. The Devil opens this chapter by stating, "Anyone who submits to annoyance by things he does not want is not definite. He is a drifter." Do you find yourself "submitting to annoyance"? If so, how often do you do so and what is the outcome?

2. The Devil goes on to say that "minds which do not harmonize should never be forced to remain together in marriage or any other relationship." He states that friction leads to drifting and indefiniteness. Give an example of this in your life or the lives of your loved ones. How did this affect you?

3. According to these teachings, your first duty should be toward yourself, that you have a duty of finding how to live a full and happy life. To what extent have you found this? On a scale of 1 to 10 (1 being "very little" and 10 being "very much so"), rate the degree to which you believe your life to be full and happy:
1 —— 2 —— 3 —— 4 —— 5 —— 6 —— 7 —— 8 —— 9 —— 10

4. Many may judge this as selfish. However, can you fully commit to serving others if you do not feel fulfilled yourself? Please explain.

5. According to the Devil, many parents struggle with a false sense of duty that in turn indulges the children, as opposed to "forcing them to seek and gain knowledge at first hand." In other words, "too much help thrust upon the youth encourages him to drift and become indefinite in all things." Do you believe this to be true? Why or why not? Use examples to substantiate your point of view.

6. Napoleon Hill states, "Unearned gifts of every nature may become a curse instead of a blessing." What do you think he means by this?

7. The Devil advocates the prayer of definiteness of purpose over empty begging and meaningless words. Do you pray? If so, how?

8. What do you believe the difference is? Have you ever prayed with definiteness of purpose? If so, what was the outcome? If not, would you be willing to try doing so?

9. The Devil asserts that "all prayers bring that for which one prays." He goes on to explain that most people pray after everything else fails them, when their fears are realized. Reflect on your life. Do you pray? If so, do you most often do so only when your fears are realized? Please explain.

10. The Devil states that transmuting one's dominating desires into their physical equivalent is all that there is to prayer. What are your thoughts regarding this statement? Does it parallel your beliefs?

11. He goes on to state that "people who whine and beg God to assume responsibility for all their troubles and provide them with all the necessities and luxuries of life are too lazy to create what they want and translate it into existence through the power of their own minds." Do you believe this to be true for you? Why or why not?

12. It is shared that definiteness is the first requisite for success. List the ways that you believe yourself to be lacking definiteness in your life.

13. It is said that negativity has the same power as omnipotence—that one cannot exist without the other. There is a balancing of the two energies. Humans have a choice as to whether they fill their brains with negativity or positivity. If this is the case, what are your thoughts about what is currently shared most in popular media? Is it mostly positive or negative? What effect do you believe it is having on the minds of the masses? Please explain.

14. According to the Devil, humans underestimate their power. Where do you currently see evidence of this in the world?

15. At that time, it was shared that children were not taught a practical working knowledge of the power of their minds and that the churches and schools did not teach people to think for themselves. Do you believe this still to be true? Why or why not?

16. The Devil asserts that "ignorance and fear are the only enemies for which men need salvation." Write a list of all that you fear. Do you believe they are the only things from which you need salvation? Please explain.

17. The Devil asserts that only two out of every one hundred people are independent thinkers. Who are the two people you know whom you believe to be independent thinkers? Please explain.

18. The Devil asserts that the school systems cram facts for "credits" into children's minds, as opposed to helping children learn how to use their minds. Do you believe this still to be true in your schools? Why or why not?

19. The Devil also speaks of how higher institutions operate entirely for the select few who are entitled and wealthy and evolves from indefiniteness of purpose. Do you still believe this to be true today? Why or why not?

20. The Devil lists the ways in which churches and schools could be modified for greater good as the following. For each, on a scale from 1 to 10 (1 being "very little" and 10 being "very much so") rate the degree to which you experienced these principles while you were in school:

Have you "lead" as opposed to follow in your schoolwork:

1 —— 2 —— 3 —— 4 —— 5 —— 6 —— 7 —— 8 —— 9 —— 10

Your instructors served as students, and you, as a student, served as the instructor:

1 —— 2 —— 3 —— 4 —— 5 —— 6 —— 7 —— 8 —— 9 —— 10

Organize schools so that you, as a student, can learn by doing, especially by engaging in "practical labor connected with the daily problems of life":

1 —— 2 —— 3 —— 4 —— 5 —— 6 —— 7 —— 8 —— 9 —— 10

You were taught to recognize practical ideas that would help you to acquire your wants and needs:

1 —— 2 —— 3 —— 4 —— 5 —— 6 —— 7 —— 8 —— 9 —— 10

You were taught how to budget and use time, valuing it as a great asset:

1 —— 2 —— 3 —— 4 —— 5 —— 6 —— 7 —— 8 —— 9 —— 10

You were taught about the basic motives by which people are influenced, and in turn how you can use that knowledge to acquire necessities and luxuries in your life:

1 —— 2 —— 3 —— 4 —— 5 —— 6 —— 7 —— 8 —— 9 —— 10

You were taught about nutrition and its relationship to maintaining a healthy life:

1 —— 2 —— 3 —— 4 —— 5 —— 6 —— 7 —— 8 —— 9 —— 10

You were taught the true nature of sex and how it can be transmuted and used toward greater achievement:

1 —— 2 —— 3 —— 4 —— 5 —— 6 —— 7 —— 8 —— 9 —— 10

You were taught and shown how to cultivate definite purpose in your life:

1 —— 2 —— 3 —— 4 —— 5 —— 6 —— 7 —— 8 —— 9 —— 10

You were taught about the nature and possibilities for good and evil, along with the principle of habit:

1 —— 2 —— 3 —— 4 —— 5 —— 6 —— 7 —— 8 —— 9 —— 10

You were taught about the law of hypnotic rhythm:

1 —— 2 —— 3 —— 4 —— 5 —— 6 —— 7 —— 8 —— 9 —— 10

In the lower grades, you cultivated habits that led you to independent thought:

1 —— 2 —— 3 —— 4 —— 5 —— 6 —— 7 —— 8 —— 9 —— 10

You were taught the difference between failure and temporary defeat:

1 —— 2 —— 3 —— 4 —— 5 —— 6 —— 7 —— 8 —— 9 —— 10

You were shown how to search for the advantages that come with every defeat:

1 —— 2 —— 3 —— 4 —— 5 —— 6 —— 7 —— 8 —— 9 —— 10

You were taught how to express your thoughts fearlessly, along with how to rely upon your own judgment, knowing how reject or accept the ideas of others:

1 —— 2 —— 3 —— 4 —— 5 —— 6 —— 7 —— 8 —— 9 —— 10

You were taught to make decisions promptly and to be slow to change them once made, unless you had definite reason to do so:

1 —— 2 —— 3 —— 4 —— 5 —— 6 —— 7 —— 8 —— 9 —— 10

You were taught the nature of the brain, and how it receives energy from nature and specializes it into definite thought, and how the brain is an instrument for the interpretation of stimuli that cause thought:

1 —— 2 —— 3 —— 4 —— 5 —— 6 —— 7 —— 8 —— 9 —— 10

You were taught the value of harmony in your mind, and how it can only be attained through self-control:

1 —— 2 —— 3 —— 4 —— 5 —— 6 —— 7 —— 8 —— 9 —— 10

You were taught the nature and value of self-control:

1 — 2 — 3 — 4 — 5 — 6 — 7 — 8 — 9 — 10

You were taught that there is a low of increasing returns, which should be put in operation as a matter of habit; this is done by rendering more and better service than is expected of you:

1 — 2 — 3 — 4 — 5 — 6 — 7 — 8 — 9 — 10

Everything you do for others, you actually do for yourself:

1 — 2 — 3 — 4 — 5 — 6 — 7 — 8 — 9 — 10

Only base your opinions on facts or beliefs that can be accepted as facts:

1 — 2 — 3 — 4 — 5 — 6 — 7 — 8 — 9 — 10

You understand that overindulging in hedonistic habits such as cigarette smoking, consuming liquor, narcotics, and sexual activity will destroy your willpower and lead you to drifting:

1 — 2 — 3 — 4 — 5 — 6 — 7 — 8 — 9 — 10

It is dangerous to blindly follow the beliefs of your parents, religious instructors, or anyone else:

1 — 2 — 3 — 4 — 5 — 6 — 7 — 8 — 9 — 10

Own your mistakes and face facts, without trying to condone yourself:

1 — 2 — 3 — 4 — 5 — 6 — 7 — 8 — 9 — 10

You have been encouraged to use your sixth sense and carefully examine all ideas that come from that sense:

1 — 2 — 3 — 4 — 5 — 6 — 7 — 8 — 9 — 10

You understand Ralph Waldo Emerson's interpretation of the law of compensation and how it works in the everyday affairs of your life:

1 — 2 — 3 — 4 — 5 — 6 — 7 — 8 — 9 — 10

The most powerful way for you to pray is with definiteness of purpose, backed by persistently and continuously applying definite plans:

1 — 2 — 3 — 4 — 5 — 6 — 7 — 8 — 9 — 10

Your value in life is measured by the quality and quantity of useful service you provide:

1 — 2 — 3 — 4 — 5 — 6 — 7 — 8 — 9 — 10

Each problem has a solution that can often be found in the circumstances that created that problem:

1 — 2 — 3 — 4 — 5 — 6 — 7 — 8 — 9 — 10

Your only problems are those that you or others set in your mind:

1 — 2 — 3 — 4 — 5 — 6 — 7 — 8 — 9 — 10

You can achieve whatever you can conceive and believe:

1 — 2 — 3 — 4 — 5 — 6 — 7 — 8 — 9 — 10

Learning from your life's experiences is the greatest schooling you can get:

1 — 2 — 3 — 4 — 5 — 6 — 7 — 8 — 9 — 10

Always be true to yourself, for you can never please everybody:

1 — 2 — 3 — 4 — 5 — 6 — 7 — 8 — 9 — 10

You learned the psychology of harmoniousness:

1 — 2 — 3 — 4 — 5 — 6 — 7 — 8 — 9 — 10

You were taught the principles of personal achievement to attain financial independence:

1 — 2 — 3 — 4 — 5 — 6 — 7 — 8 — 9 — 10

You were instructed in groups and in round-table format, with individual instruction with subjects that could not be properly taught to you in groups:

1 — 2 — 3 — 4 — 5 — 6 — 7 — 8 — 9 — 10

You were also taught by professionals (scientists, artists, engineers, and media experts) who instilled in you the practical working knowledge of their crafts:

1 — 2 — 3 — 4 — 5 — 6 — 7 — 8 — 9 — 10

21. The Devil goes on to name the common forms of sin. Reflect on your life, and on a scale from 1 to 10 (1 being "very little" and 10 being "very much so"), note how much you indulged in these behaviors.

    Overeating:

    1 — 2 — 3 — 4 — 5 — 6 — 7 — 8 — 9 — 10

    Overindulging in sex:

    1 — 2 — 3 — 4 — 5 — 6 — 7 — 8 — 9 — 10

Allow your mind to be dominated by negative thoughts of envy:
1 — 2 — 3 — 4 — 5 — 6 — 7 — 8 — 9 — 10

Allow your mind to be dominated by negative thoughts of greed:
1 — 2 — 3 — 4 — 5 — 6 — 7 — 8 — 9 — 10

Allow your mind to be dominated by negative thoughts of fear:
1 — 2 — 3 — 4 — 5 — 6 — 7 — 8 — 9 — 10

Allow your mind to be dominated by negative thoughts of hatred:
1 — 2 — 3 — 4 — 5 — 6 — 7 — 8 — 9 — 10

Allow your mind to be dominated by negative thoughts of tolerance:
1 — 2 — 3 — 4 — 5 — 6 — 7 — 8 — 9 — 10

Allow your mind to be dominated by negative thoughts of vanity:
1 — 2 — 3 — 4 — 5 — 6 — 7 — 8 — 9 — 10

Allow your mind to be dominated by negative thoughts of self-pity:
1 — 2 — 3 — 4 — 5 — 6 — 7 — 8 — 9 — 10

Allow your mind to be dominated by negative thoughts of discouragement:
1 — 2 — 3 — 4 — 5 — 6 — 7 — 8 — 9 — 10

Allow your mind to be dominated by negative thoughts of envy:
1 — 2 — 3 — 4 — 5 — 6 — 7 — 8 — 9 — 10

Cheating:
1 — 2 — 3 — 4 — 5 — 6 — 7 — 8 — 9 — 10

Lying:
1 — 2 — 3 — 4 — 5 — 6 — 7 — 8 — 9 — 10

Stealing:
1 — 2 — 3 — 4 — 5 — 6 — 7 — 8 — 9 — 10

Remaining in ignorance:
1 — 2 — 3 — 4 — 5 — 6 — 7 — 8 — 9 — 10

Neglect by accepting that which you don't want in your life:
1 — 2 — 3 — 4 — 5 — 6 — 7 — 8 — 9 — 10

Drifting through life without definite plans and purpose:

1 —— 2 —— 3 —— 4 —— 5 —— 6 —— 7 —— 8 —— 9 —— 10

22. The Devil defines faith as "a state of mind wherein one recognizes and uses the power of positive thought as a medium by which one contacts and draws upon the universal storehouse of infinite intelligence at will." On a scale from 1 to 10 (1 being "very little" and 10 being "very much so"), rate how much faith you believe yourself to currently have:

1 —— 2 —— 3 —— 4 —— 5 —— 6 —— 7 —— 8 —— 9 —— 10

23. After reflecting on your life and the ratings that you provided, what do you believe to be the areas in which you could most improve to support greater definite purpose and focus in your life?

Chapter 10

Self-Discipline

Q What preparation must one undergo before being able to move with definiteness of purpose at all times?
    A. One must gain *mastery over self*. This is the second of the seven principles. The person who is not master of himself can never be master of others. Lack of self-mastery is, of itself, the most destructive form of indefiniteness.

Q Where should one begin when making a start at control over self?
    A. By mastering the three appetites responsible for most of one's lack of self-discipline. The three appetites are (1) the desire for food, (2) the desire for expression of sex, (3) the desire to express loosely organized opinions.

Q Does man have other appetites which need control?
    A. Yes, many of them, but these three are the ones which should be conquered first. When a man becomes master of these three appetites, he has developed enough self-discipline to conquer easily those of lesser importance.

Q But these are natural appetites. They must be indulged if one is to be healthy and happy.

A. To be sure they are natural appetites, but they are also dangerous because people who have not mastered themselves overfeed the appetites. Self-mastery contemplates sufficient control over the appetites to enable one to feed them what they need and withhold food not needed.

Q Your viewpoint is both interesting and educational. Describe the details through which I may understand how and under what circumstances people over-feed the appetites.

A. Take the desire for physical food, for example. The majority of people are so weak in self-discipline they fill their stomachs with combinations of rich food which please the taste but overwork the organs of digestion and elimination.

They pour into their stomachs both quantity and combinations of food which the body chemist can dispose of only by converting the food into deadly toxic poisons.

These poisons clog and stagnate the body sewer system until it slows down in its work of elimination of waste matter. After a while the sewer system stops working altogether, and the victim has what he calls "constipation."

By that time he is ready for the hospital. Auto-intoxication, or body sewer poisoning, takes the machinery of the brain and rolls it into something resembling a wad of putty.

The victim then becomes sluggish in his physical movements and mentally irritable and fussy. If he could only take one good look at, and one bad smell of, his sewer system, he would be ashamed to look himself in the face.

City sewers are not the pleasantest of places when they become over-loaded or clogged, but they are clean and sweet compared with the intestinal sewer when it has been overloaded or clogged. This is not a pretty story to be associated with the pleasant and necessary act of eating, but that is where it belongs because overeating and wrong food combinations are the evils which cause auto-intoxication.

People who eat wisely and keep their body sewers clean handicap me because a clean body sewer generally means a sound body and a brain that functions properly.

Imagine—if your imagination can be stretched that far how any human being could move with definiteness of purpose with his body sewer filled with enough poison to kill a hundred people if it were injected into their bloodstream directly.

Q. And all this trouble is the result of lack of control over the physical appetite for food?

A. Well, if you wish to be absolutely correct you should say that improper eating is responsible for the majority of the ills of the body, and practically all headaches.

If you want proof of this, select 100 people suffering with headaches and give each of them a thorough washing out of their body sewer systems with a high enema, and observe that no fewer than ninety-five of the headaches will disappear within a few minutes after their sewers have been cleaned.

Q. From all you say about the intestinal tract, I gather the impression that mastery over the physical appetite for food means also mastery over the habit of neglecting to keep the intestines clean.

A. Yes, that is true. It is just as important to eliminate the waste matter of the body and the unused portions of food as it is to take the right amount and the correct combinations of food.

Q. I never thought of auto-intoxication as being one of your devices of control over people, and I am utterly shocked to know how many people are victims of this subtle enemy. Let's hear what you have to say of the other two appetites.

A. Well, take the desire for sex expression. Now there is a force with which I master the weak and the strong, the old and the young, the ignorant and the wise. In fact, I master all who neglect to master sex!

Q How can one master the emotion of sex?
A. By the simple process of transmuting that emotion into some form of activity other than copulation. Sex is one of the greatest of all forces which motivate human beings. Because of this fact it is also one of the most dangerous forces. If humans would control their sex desires and transmute them into a driving force with which to carry on their occupation—that is, if they spent on their work one half the time they dissipate in pursuit of sex, they would never know poverty.

Q Do I understand you to imply there is a relationship between sex and poverty?
A. Yes, where sex is not under definite control. If allowed to run its natural course, sex will quickly lead one into the habit of drifting.

Q Is there any relationship between sex and leadership?
A. Yes, all great leaders in every walk of life are highly sexed, but they follow the habit of controlling their sex desires, switching them into a driving force behind their occupation.

Q Is the habit of over-indulgence in sex as dangerous as the habit of taking narcotics or liquor?
A. There is no difference between these habits. Both lead to hypnotic control, through the habit of drifting!

Q Why does the world look upon sex as something vulgar?
A. Because of the vulgar abuse people have made of this emotion. It is not sex that is vulgar. It is the individual who neglects or refuses to control and guide it.

Q. Do you mean, by your statement, that one should not indulge the desire for sex?

A. No, I mean that sex, like all other forces available to man, should be understood, mastered, and made to serve man. The desire for sex expression is as natural as the desire for food. The desire can no more be killed than one can entirely stop a river from flowing. If the emotion of sex is shut off from the natural mode of expression, it will break out in some other less desirable form, just as a river will, if dammed, break through and flow around the dam. The person who has self-discipline understands the emotion of sex, respects it, and learns to control and transmute it into constructive activities.

Q. Just what damage is there in over-indulgence of sex?

A. The greatest damage is that it depletes the source of man's greatest driving force, and wastes, without adequate compensation, man's creative energy.

It dissipates energy needed by nature to maintain physical health. Sex is nature's most useful therapeutic force.

It depletes the magnetic energy which is the source of an attractive, pleasing personality.

It removes the sparkle from one's eyes and sets up discord in the tone of one's voice.

It destroys enthusiasm, subdues ambition, and leads inevitably to the habit of drifting on all subjects.

Q. I would like for you to answer my question in another way by telling me what beneficial ends the emotion of sex may be made to attain, if mastered and transmuted.

A. Controlled sex supplies the magnetic force that attracts people to one another. It is the most important factor of a pleasing personality.

It gives quality to the tone of voice and enables one to convey through the voice any feeling desired.

It serves, as nothing else can serve, to give motive-power to one's desires.

It keeps the nervous system charged with the energy needed to carry on the work of maintaining the body.

It sharpens the imagination and enables one to create useful ideas.

It gives quickness and definiteness to one's physical and mental movements.

It gives one persistence and perseverance in the pursuit of one's major purpose in life.

It is a great antidote for all fear.

It gives one immunity against discouragement. It helps to master laziness and procrastination.

It gives one physical and mental endurance while undergoing any form of opposition or defeat.

It gives one the fighting qualities necessary under all circumstances for self-defense.

In brief, it makes winners and not quitters!

Q. Are those all the advantages you claim for controlled sex energy?

A. No, they are only some of the more important benefits it provides.

Perhaps some will believe the greatest of all the virtues of sex is that it is nature's method of perpetuation of all living things. This alone should remove all thought that sex is vulgar.

Q. I gather, from what you say, that the emotion of sex is a virtue, not a fault.

A. It is a virtue when controlled and directed to the attainment of desirable ends. It is a fault when neglected and permitted to lead to acts of lust.

Q **Why aren't these truths taught to children by their parents and the public schools?**
A. The neglect is due to ignorance of the real nature of sex.

It is just as necessary in maintaining health for one to understand and properly use the emotion of sex as it is to keep the body sewer system clean. Both subjects should be taught in all public schools and all homes where there are children.

Q **Wouldn't the majority of parents need instruction on the proper function and use of sex before they could intelligently teach their children?**
A. Yes, and so would the public schoolteachers.

Q **What relative position of importance would you give to the need for accurate knowledge on the subject of sex?**
A. It is next to the top of the list. There is but one thing of greater importance to human beings. That is accurate thought.

Q **Do I understand you to say that knowledge of the true functions of sex and ability to think accurately are the two things of greatest importance to mankind?**
A. That is what I intended you to understand. Accurate thinking comes first because it is the solution to all man's problems, the answer to all his prayers, the source of opulence and all material possessions. Accurate thinking is aided by properly controlled and directed sex emotion because sex emotion is the same energy as that with which one thinks. It begins with those who desire self-determination sufficiently to be willing to pay its price. No one can be entirely free—spiritually, mentally, physically, and economically—without learning the art of accurate thinking. No one can learn to think accurately without including, as a part of the needed knowledge, information on the control of sex emotion through transmutation.

Q It will be a great surprise to many people to learn there is so close a relationship between thinking and sex emotion. Tell us, now, about the third appetite, and let's see what it has to do with self-discipline.

A. The habit of expressing loosely organized opinions is one of the most destructive of habits. Its destructiveness consists in its tendency to influence people to guess instead of searching for the facts when they form opinions, create ideas, or organize plans.

The habit develops a grasshopper mind—one that jumps from one thing to another but never completes anything.

And of course, carelessness in the expression of opinions leads to the habit of drifting. From there it is only a step or two until one is bound by the law of hypnotic rhythm which automatically prohibits accurate thinking.

Q What other disadvantages are there in free expression of opinions?

A. The person who talks too much informs the world of his aims and plans and gives to others the opportunity to profit by his ideas.

Wise men keep their plans to themselves and refrain from expressing uninvited opinions. This prevents others from appropriating their ideas and makes it difficult for others to interfere with their plans.

Q Why do so many people indulge in the habit of expressing uninvited opinions?

A. The habit is one way of expressing egotism and vanity. The desire for self-expression is inborn in people. The motive behind the habit is to attract the attention of others and to impress them favorably. Actually it has just the opposite effect. When the self-invited speaker attracts attention, it usually is unfavorable.

Q. Yes, what other disadvantages has the habit?
A. The person who insists on talking seldom has an opportunity to learn by listening to others.

Q. But isn't it true that a magnetic speaker often puts himself in the way of opportunity to benefit himself by attracting the attention of others through his powers of oratory?
A. Yes, a magnetic orator does have an asset of tremendous value in his ability to impress people by his speech, but he cannot make the best use of this asset if he forces his speech on others without their invitation.

No single quality adds more to one's personality than the ability to speak with emotional feeling, force, and conviction, but the speaker must not impose his speech upon others without being invited to do so. There is an old saying that nothing is worth more than its actual cost. This applies as well to the free uninvited expression of opinions as to material things.

Q. What about people who volunteer their opinions by expressing them in writing? Do they also suffer by lack of self-discipline?
A. One of the worst pests on earth is the person who writes uninvited letters to people of prominence. Men in public office, moving picture stars, men who have succeeded in business or written a best-selling book, and people whose names appear often in the newspapers are continuously besieged by people who write letters expressing their opinion on all subjects.

Q. But the writing of uninvited letters is a harmless way of finding pleasure through self-expression, is it not? What damage does one do by the habit?
A. Habits are contagious. Every habit attracts a flock of its relatives. The habit of doing anything that is useless leads to the formation of other habits that are useless, especially the habit of drifting.

But that is not all the dangers associated with the habit of indulging in uninvited expression of opinions. The habit creates enemies and places in their hands dangerous weapons by which they may do great injury to the one who indulges in it. Thieves and confidence men and racketeers pay big prices for the names and addresses of the writers of uninvited letters, knowing as they do the writers of these letters become easy victims of all manner of schemes that result in the loss of their money. They refer to the writers of such letters as "nuts." If you wish to know how foolish people are who write uninvited letters, read the "nut column" of any newspaper—the column in which the paper publishes the voluntary opinions of its readers—and you will see for yourself how the writers of such letters antagonize people and invite opposition from others.

Q. I had no idea, Your Majesty, that people get into so much difficulty through uninvited expression of their opinions, but now that you have brought up the subject I do remember writing the editor of a prominent magazine an uninvited letter of criticism which cost me a fine position on his staff, at a fat salary.

A. That is a perfect example. The proper place to begin self-discipline is right where you stand. The way to begin is by recognizing the truth—that there is nothing for good or evil throughout the myriads of universes except the power of natural law. There is no individual personality anywhere throughout the myriad of universes with the slightest power to influence a human being save nature and human beings themselves.

There is no human being now living, no human being has ever lived, and no human being ever will live with the right or the power to deprive another human being of the inborn privilege of free and independent thought. That privilege is the only one over which any human being can have absolute control. No adult human being ever loses the right to freedom of thought, but most humans lose the benefits of this privilege either by neglect or because it has been taken away from them by their parents or religious instructors before the age of understanding. These are self-evident truths, no less important because they are being called to your attention by the Devil than they would be if brought to your attention by my opposition.

Q. But what are people going to lean upon in the hour of emergency when they know not where nor to whom to appeal?

A. Let them lean upon the only dependable power available to any human being.

Q. And what is that?

A. Themselves! The power of their own thoughts. The only power they can control and may rely upon. The only power which cannot be perverted, colored, modified, and falsified by their dishonest fellow human beings.

Q. All you say seems logical, but why must I come to the Devil to discover such profound truths? Let's get back to the seven principles. You have already disclosed enough information to show clearly that the secret of how to break the power of hypnotic rhythm is wrapped in the seven principles. You have shown, too, that the most important of these principles is self-discipline. Now go ahead and describe the other five principles you have not yet mentioned, and indicate what part they play in giving one self-discipline.

A. First, let me summarize that part of my confession we have already covered.

I have frankly told you that my two most effective devices for mastering human beings are the habit of drifting and the law of hypnotic rhythm. I have shown you that drifting is not a natural law, but a man-made habit which leads to man's submission to the law of hypnotic rhythm.

The seven principles are the media by which man may break the hold of hypnotic rhythm and take possession, again, of his own mind.

You see, therefore, the seven principles are the seven steps which lead victims of hypnotic rhythm out of the self-made prisons in which they are bound.

Q. The seven principles are the master key that unlocks the door to spiritual, mental, and economic self-determination? Is that true?

A. Yes, that's another way of stating the truth.

STUDY GUIDE

Chapter 10:
Self-Discipline

1. This chapter opens with a discussion about the preparation one must undertake before being able to move with definite purpose. To do so, you must first gain mastery over yourself. Before delving further, what do you think this means specifically? How does one gain mastery over themselves?

2. The Devil outlines that there are three appetites responsible for one's lack of self-discipline: (1) the desire for food, (2) the desire for expression of sex, and (3) the desire to express loosely organized opinions. Napoleon Hill responds that these are all natural appetites, but the Devil responds that these appetites are most often overfed. On a scale from 1 to 10 (1 being "very little" and 10 being "very much so"), rate how much you believe yourself to overindulge.

   Desire for food:
   1 —— 2 —— 3 —— 4 —— 5 —— 6 —— 7 —— 8 —— 9 —— 10

   Desire for sexual expression:
   1 —— 2 —— 3 —— 4 —— 5 —— 6 —— 7 —— 8 —— 9 —— 10

   Desire to express loosely organized opinions:
   1 —— 2 —— 3 —— 4 —— 5 —— 6 —— 7 —— 8 —— 9 —— 10

3. Do you believe that you often overfill your stomach with rich foods that overwork your digestive organs? Please explain.

4. On a scale from 1 to 10 (1 being "very little" and 10 being "very much so"), rate how much you suffer from constipation:
   1 —— 2 —— 3 —— 4 —— 5 —— 6 —— 7 —— 8 —— 9 —— 10

5. While the inner workings of the digestive system are described in very basic terms, the ultimate issues stated were sluggishness, irritability,

and fussiness. Do you suffer from any of these ailments? If so, do you attribute them in any way to the food that you eat? Please explain.

6. The Devil goes on to share that 95 out of 100 people suffer from headaches because their bodily sewer systems need to be cleaned. Do you believe that you have previously suffered from "auto-intoxication." If so, how did you cure it? If not, are you committed to curing it?

7. Mastering the emotion of sex involves transmuting your sexual desires and using that energy toward occupational endeavors. Do you believe that you obsess over sex in a way that distracts you from greater success? Please explain.

8. The Devil claims that "all great leaders in every walk of life are highly sexed, but they follow the habit of controlling their sex desires, switching them into a driving force behind their occupation." Do you believe this to be true? Please cite examples in your life or among the acclaimed leaders whom you admire.

9. The Devil claims that sex itself is not vulgar, but the individual who neglects or refuses to control and guide it is. Do you see evidence of this in the world?

10. The Devil claims that man loses his creative energy if he puts too much focus and energy into sexual pursuits. Have you ever found yourself obsessive about sex or anything else to the point where you believe it has interfered with your creative energy? If so, please explain and describe how you were able to shift it (or not).

11. He also claims that sexual obsession dissipates energy needed to maintain physical health and depletes one's charisma or magnetism. How do you believe it might do so?

12. It is claimed that controlled sex has many benefits. On a scale from 1 to 10 (1 being "very little" and 10 being "very much so"), rate yourself on how much you have mastered each of these traits:

Having a pleasing personality:
1 —— 2 —— 3 —— 4 —— 5 —— 6 —— 7 —— 8 —— 9 —— 10

Having a quality tone of voice:
1 —— 2 —— 3 —— 4 —— 5 —— 6 —— 7 —— 8 —— 9 —— 10

Being motivated:
1 —— 2 —— 3 —— 4 —— 5 —— 6 —— 7 —— 8 —— 9 —— 10

Having an energized nervous system:
1 — 2 — 3 — 4 — 5 — 6 — 7 — 8 — 9 — 10

Having a sharp imagination:
1 — 2 — 3 — 4 — 5 — 6 — 7 — 8 — 9 — 10

Having physical and mental quickness:
1 — 2 — 3 — 4 — 5 — 6 — 7 — 8 — 9 — 10

Having a pleasing personality:
1 — 2 — 3 — 4 — 5 — 6 — 7 — 8 — 9 — 10

Having persistence and perseverance:
1 — 2 — 3 — 4 — 5 — 6 — 7 — 8 — 9 — 10

Are unencumbered by fear:
1 — 2 — 3 — 4 — 5 — 6 — 7 — 8 — 9 — 10

Are immune to discouragement:
1 — 2 — 3 — 4 — 5 — 6 — 7 — 8 — 9 — 10

Master laziness and procrastination:
1 — 2 — 3 — 4 — 5 — 6 — 7 — 8 — 9 — 10

Have physical and mental endurance:
1 — 2 — 3 — 4 — 5 — 6 — 7 — 8 — 9 — 10

Exhibit strong abilities in self-defense:
1 — 2 — 3 — 4 — 5 — 6 — 7 — 8 — 9 — 10

13. It is emphasized that sexual control is a virtue and not a fault. Were you raised to believe that any sexual expression was bad or evil? Describe the beliefs you were raised with and how they affect your energy around sex.

14. Sex becomes a fault when it is (1) neglected and (2) permitted to lead to acts of lust. Do you often experience either?

15. Both sex and healthy eating should be taught at home and in the schools. Do you believe you were adequately taught about each in your youth?

16. Based on the dialogue between Napoleon Hill and the Devil, how do you define accurate thinking?

17. Expressing "loosely organized opinions" influences people to guess instead of searching for facts. Can you give three examples of times when you or someone you know expressed loosely organized opinions and influenced others accordingly.

18. Do you ever suffer from grasshopper mind? If so, when do you find yourself behaving in this way?

19. It is shared that "the person who talks too much informs the world of his aims and plans and gives to others the opportunity to profit by his ideas." Have you ever shared too much or too many of your ideas, to your own detriment? If so, please explain.

20. On a scale from 1 to 10 (1 being "very little" and 10 being "very much so"), rate how much you get lost in egoic thinking:

    1 —— 2 —— 3 —— 4 —— 5 —— 6 —— 7 —— 8 —— 9 —— 10

21. On a scale from 1 to 10 (1 being "very little" and 10 being "very much so"), rate how vain you believe yourself to be:

    1 —— 2 —— 3 —— 4 —— 5 —— 6 —— 7 —— 8 —— 9 —— 10

22. It is shared that when the self-invited speaker attracts attention, it is most often unfavorable. Where have you seen evidence of this?

23. The person who insists on talking often misses the opportunity to learn by listening. On a scale from 1 to 10 (1 being "very little" and 10 being "very much so"), rate your ability as an active listener:

    1 —— 2 —— 3 —— 4 —— 5 —— 6 —— 7 —— 8 —— 9 —— 10

24. On a scale from 1 to 10 (1 being "very little" and 10 being "very much so"), rate yourself as an inspiring and effective speaker:

    1 —— 2 —— 3 —— 4 —— 5 —— 6 —— 7 —— 8 —— 9 —— 10

25. Do you most often wait to be invited before speaking? If not, do you find there are times when your charisma is less because you are imposing yourself on others? Please explain.

26. On a scale from 1 to 10 (1 being "very little" and 10 being "very much so"), rate how much you get lost in egoic thinking:

    1 —— 2 —— 3 —— 4 —— 5 —— 6 —— 7 —— 8 —— 9 —— 10

27. Do you ever indulge in uninvited expressions of opinion through writing letters, emails, or other forms of communication? Especially with social media, many are spending a great deal of time and energy engaging in listing grievances and negative opinions. Do you do so?

Do you believe such expressions affect both the writer and the readers? Please explain.

28. Writing negativity antagonizes people and invites opposition from others. Napoleon Hill shared how he lost a position as a member of a magazine's staff because he wrote a letter to the editor. Have you ever suffered in response to communicating in a negative way? Please explain.

Chapter 11

Learning from Adversity

Q Is failure ever a benefit to man?
A. Yes. Indeed, learning from adversity is the third of the seven principles. But few people know that every adversity brings with it the seed of an equivalent advantage. Still fewer people know the difference between temporary defeat and failure. If this knowledge were generally known, I would be deprived of one of my strongest weapons of control over human beings.

Q But I understood you to say that failure is one of your greatest allies. I got the impression from your confession that failure causes people to lose ambition and quit trying, and then you take them over without opposition on their part.
A. That is just the point. I take them over after they quit trying. If they knew the difference between temporary defeat and failure, they would not quit when they meet with opposition from life. If they knew that every form of defeat, and all failures, bring with them the seed of unborn opportunity, they would keep on fighting and win. Success usually is but one short step beyond the point where one quits fighting.

Q. Is that all one might learn from adversity, defeat, and failure?

A. No, that is the least of what one might learn. I hate to tell you this, but failure often serves as a blessing in disguise because it breaks the grip of hypnotic rhythm and frees the mind for a fresh start.

Q. Now we are getting somewhere. So you have confessed, at long last, that even nature's law of hypnotic rhythm can be and often is annulled by nature herself. Is that correct?

A. No, that is not stating the matter accurately. Nature never reverses any of her natural laws. Nature does not take away a human being's freedom of thought through hypnotic rhythm. The individual gives up his freedom by abuse of this law. If a man jumped from a tree and was killed by the sudden impact of his body with the earth, through the law of gravity, you wouldn't say nature murdered him, would you? You would say the man neglected to relate himself properly to the law of gravity.

Q. I am beginning to see. The law of hypnotic rhythm is capable of both negative and positive application. It may drag one down to slavery through loss of the privilege of freedom of thought, or it may help one rise to great heights of achievement through the free use of thought, depending on how the individual relates himself to the law. Is that correct?

A. Now you have it right.

Q. But what about failure? One does not fail intentionally, with purpose aforethought. No one encourages temporary defeat. These are circumstances over which the individual often has no control whatsoever. How, then, can it be said that nature does not take away one's freedom of thought when failure destroys ambition, will power, and the self-confidence essential to make a fresh start?

A. Failure is a man-made circumstance. It is never real until it has been accepted by man as permanent. Stating it another way, failure is a state of mind; therefore, it is something an individual can control until he neglects to exercise this privilege. Nature does not force people to fail. But nature does impose her law of hypnotic rhythm upon all minds and through this law gives permanency to the thoughts which dominate those minds.

In other words, failure thoughts are taken over by the law of hypnotic rhythm and made permanent if the individual accepts any circumstances as being permanent failure. That same law just as readily takes over and makes permanent thoughts of success.

Q What part, then, does failure play in helping an individual break the grip of hypnotic rhythm after that law has been fastened upon his mind?

A. Failure brings a climax in which one has the privilege of clearing his mind of fear and making a new start in another direction. Failure proves conclusively that something is wrong with one's aims or the plans by which the object of these aims is sought. Failure is the dead end of the habit-path one has been following, and when it is reached it forces one to leave that path and take up another, thereby creating a new rhythm.

But failure does more than this. It gives an individual an opportunity to test himself wherein he may learn how much will power he possesses. Failure also forces people to learn many truths they would never discover without it. Failure often leads an individual to an understanding of the power of self-discipline without which no one could turn back after having once been the victim of hypnotic rhythm.

Study the lives of all people who achieve outstanding success in any calling and observe, with profit, that their success is usually in exact ratio to their experiences of defeat before succeeding.

Q Is this all you have to say of the advantages of failure?

A. No, I have barely begun. If you want the real significance of adversity, failure, defeat, and all other experiences which break up a human being's habits and force him to form new habits, watch nature at her work. Nature uses illness to break the physical rhythm of the body when the cells and organs become improperly related. She uses economic depressions to break the rhythm of mass thought when great numbers of people become improperly related—through business, social, and political activities. And she uses failure to break the rhythm of negative thought when an individual becomes improperly related to himself in his own mind.

Observe carefully and you will see that everywhere in nature there is always at work a natural law which gives eternal change to all matter, all energy, and to the power of thought. The only permanent thing in the universes is change. Eternal, inexorable change—through which every atom of matter and every unit of energy has the opportunity to properly relate itself to all other units of matter and energy, and every human being has the opportunity and the privilege of properly relating himself to all other human beings no matter how many mistakes he makes, or how many times or in what ways he may be defeated.

When mass failure overtakes a nation, such as the 1929 world business depression, the circumstance is in perfect harmony with nature's plan to break up man's habits and give out fresh opportunities.

Q **What you are saying intrigues me. Am I to understand that hypnotic rhythm has something to do with the way people relate themselves to one another?**

A. That abstract, elusive thing called character is nothing but a manifestation of the law of hypnotic rhythm; therefore, when speaking of one's character it would be proper to say his thought-habits have been crystallized into a positive or a negative personality, through hypnotic rhythm. One is good or bad because of the knitting together of his thoughts and deeds through hypnotic rhythm. One is bound by poverty or blessed with abundance because his aims, plans, and desires, or lack of them, have been made permanent and real by hypnotic rhythm.

Q. Is that all you have to say of the connection between hypnotic rhythm and human relationships?

A. No, I have just begun. Remember while I am talking I am speaking of the influence of hypnotic rhythm in connection with all human relationships. Men who succeed in business do so entirely because of the way they relate themselves to their associates and to others outside of the business.

Professional men who succeed do so largely because of the manner in which they relate themselves to their clients. It is much more important for the lawyer to know people and to know the laws of nature than it is to know the law. And the doctor is a failure before he starts unless he knows how to relate himself to his patients so as to establish their faith in him.

Marriage succeeds or fails entirely because of the manner in which the participants relate themselves to one another. Proper relationship in marriage begins with a proper motive for the marriage. Most marriages do not bring happiness because the contracting parties neither understand, nor attempt to understand, the law of hypnotic rhythm, through the operation of which every word they speak, every act in which they engage, and every motive by which they are inspired to deal with each other is picked up and woven into a web that entangles them in controversial misery or gives to them the wings of freedom through which they soar above all forms of unhappiness.

Every newly made acquaintanceship between people ripens into friendship and then into spiritual harmony (sometimes called love) or plants a germ of suspicion and doubt which evolves and grows into open rebellion, according to the way in which the participants in the acquaintanceship relate themselves to one another.

Hypnotic rhythm picks up the dominating motives, aims, purposes, and feelings of the contacting minds and weaves these into some degree of faith or fear, love or hatred. After the pattern has taken definite shape, as it does with time, it is forced upon the contacting minds and made a part thereof.

In this silent way does nature make permanent the dominating factors of every human relationship. In every human relationship the evil motives and the evil deeds of the contacting individuals are coordinated and consolidated into definite form and subtly woven into that all-important human trait known as character. In the same manner, the motives and the deeds of good are consolidated and forced upon the individual. You see, therefore, it is not only one's deeds but also one's very thoughts which determine the nature of all human relationships.

Q. You are leading into pretty deep water. Let's keep near the shore, where I can follow you without fear of getting beyond a safe depth. Go ahead and tell me how this subject of human relationships actually works in the current affairs of a problem filled world such as we have today.

A. That is a happy thought. But let me make sure you understand the principles I am telling about, before I try to show you how to apply them in the affairs of life.

I wish to be sure you understand that the law of hypnotic rhythm is something that no one can control, influence, or evade. But everyone can relate himself to this law so as to benefit by its inexorable operation.

Harmonious relationship with the law consists entirely of the individual changing his habits so they represent the circumstances and the things the individual wants and is willing to accept.

No one can change the law of hypnotic rhythm any more than one can change the law of gravity, but everyone can change himself. Remember, therefore, in all the discussion of this subject that all human relationships are made and maintained by the habits of the individuals related. The law of hypnotic rhythm plays only the part of solidifying the factors which constitute human relationships, but it does not create those factors. Before we go further with the discussion of human relationships, I want you to get a clear understanding of the subconscious mind.

The term "subconscious mind" represents a hypothetical physical organ which has no actual existence. The mind of man consists of universal energy (some call it Infinite Intelligence) which the individual receives, appropriates, and organizes in definite thought forms through the network of intricate physical apparatus known as a brain.

These thought forms are replicas of various stimuli which reach the brain through the five commonly known physical senses and the sixth sense, which is not so well known. When any form of stimuli reaches the brain and takes the definite shape of thought, it is classified and stored away in a group of the brain cells known as the memory group.

All thoughts of a similar nature are stored together so that the bringing forth of one leads to easy contact with all its associates. The system is very similar to the modern office filing cabinet, and it is operated in a similar manner.

The thought impressions with which one mixes the greatest amount of emotion (or feeling) are the dominating factors of the brain because they are always near the surface—at the top of the filing system, so to speak—where they spring into action voluntarily, the moment an individual neglects to exercise self-discipline. These emotion-laden thoughts are so powerful they often cause an individual to rush into action and indulge in deeds which have not been submitted to or approved by his reasoning faculty. These emotional outbursts usually destroy harmony in all human relationships. The brain often brings together combinations of emotional feeling so powerful they completely set aside the control of the reasoning faculty. On all such occasions human relationships are apt to be lacking in harmony.

Through the operation of the sixth sense, the brain of a human being may contact the filing cabinet of other brains and inspect at will whatever thought impressions are on file there. The condition under which one person may contact and inspect the filing cabinet of another person's brain is generally known as harmony, but you may better understand what is meant if I say brains attuned to the same rate of thought vibrations can easily and quickly exercise the privilege of entering and inspecting each other's filing cabinets of thoughts.

In addition to receiving organized thoughts from the filing cabinets of other brains through the sixth sense, one can, through this same physical organ, contact and receive information from the universal storehouse known as Infinite Intelligence.

All information reaching one's brain through the sixth sense comes from sources not easily isolated or traced; therefore, this sort of information is generally believed to come from one's subconscious mind. The sixth sense is the organ of the brain through which one receives all information, all knowledge, all thought impressions which do not come through one or more of the five physical senses.

Now that you understand how the mind operates, you will more easily understand how and why people come to grief through improper human relationships. You will also understand how human relationship may be made to yield riches in their highest form, riches in material, mental, and spiritual estates.

Moreover, you will understand there can never be happiness except through understanding and application of the right principles of human relationships. You will understand, too, that no individual is an entity unto himself, that completeness of mind can be attained only by harmony of purpose and deed between two or more minds. You will understand why every human being should, of his own choice, become his brother's keeper in fact as well as in theory.

Q What you say may be true, but I still insist that you have me beyond safe depths of thought. Let us get back nearer to the shore, where I can wade in familiar water. We shall go out into the deeper water after we learn to swim well. We started out to discuss the subject of how to profit by adversity, but it seems we have drifted somewhat afield from that subject.

A. We have detoured, but we have not drifted. The Devil never drifts.

The detour was necessary in order that you might be prepared to understand the most important part of this entire interview.

We are now ready to get back to the discussion of the subject of adversity. Inasmuch as most adversities grow out of improper relationships between people, it seems important to understand how people may become properly related.

Naturally the question arises as to what is a proper relationship between people? The answer is that the proper relationship is one that brings to all connected with it, or affected by it, some form of benefit.

Q What, then, is an improper relationship?
A. Any relationship between people which damages anyone or brings any form of misery or unhappiness to any of the individuals.

Q How can improper relationships be corrected?
A. By change of mind of the person causing the improper relationship, or by changing the persons to the relationship. Some minds harmonize naturally while others just as naturally clash. Successful human relationships, to endure as such, must be formed of minds that naturally harmonize, quite aside from the question of having common interests as a means of bringing them into harmony.

When you speak of business leaders who succeed because "they know how to pick men," you might more correctly say they succeed because they know how to associate minds which harmonize naturally. Knowing how to pick people successfully for any definite purpose in life is based upon ability to recognize the types of people whose minds naturally harmonize.

Q Stay focused on adversity, if you will. If there are possible benefits to be found through adversity, name some of them.
A. Adversity relieves people of vanity and egotism. It discourages selfishness by proving that no one can succeed without the cooperation of others.

Adversity forces an individual to test his mental, physical, and spiritual strength; it thus brings him face to face with his weaknesses and gives him the opportunity to bridge them.

Adversity forces one to seek ways and means to definite ends by meditation and introspective thought. This often leads to the discovery and use of the sixth sense through which one may communicate with Infinite Intelligence.

Adversity forces one to recognize the need for intelligence not available except from sources outside of one's own mind.

Adversity breaks old habits of thought and gives one an opportunity to form new habits; therefore, it may serve to break the hold of hypnotic rhythm and change its operation from negative to positive ends.

Q. What is the greatest benefit one may receive through adversity.

A. The greatest benefit of adversity is that it may, and generally does, force one to change one's thought-habits, thus breaking and redirecting the force of hypnotic rhythm.

Q. In other words, failure always is a blessing when it forces one to acquire knowledge or to build habits that lead to the achievement of one's major purpose in life. Is that correct?

A. Yes, and something more! Failure is a blessing when it forces one to depend less upon material forces and more upon spiritual forces.

Many human beings discover their "other selves," the forces which operate through the power of thought, only after some catastrophe deprives them of the full and free use of their physical bodies. When a man can no longer use his hands and his feet, he usually begins to use his brain; thus he puts himself in the way of discovering the power of his own mind.

Q What benefits may be derived from the loss of material things—money, for example?
A. The loss of material things may teach many needed lessons, none greater, however, than the truth that man has control over nothing and has no assurance of the permanent use of anything except his own power of thought.

Q I wonder if this is not the greatest benefit available through adversity?
A. No, the greatest potential benefit of any circumstance which causes one to make a fresh start is that it provides an opportunity to break the grip of hypnotic rhythm and set up a new set of thought-habits. New habits offer the only way out for people who fail. Most people who escape from the negative to the positive operation of the law of hypnotic rhythm do so only because of some form of adversity which forces them to change their thought-habits.

Q Isn't adversity apt to break one's self-reliance and cause one to give up hope?
A. It has that effect on those whose will power is weak through long established habits of drifting. It has the opposite effect on those who have not been weakened through drifting. The non-drifter meets with temporary defeat and failure, but his reaction to all forms of adversity is positive. He fights instead of giving up, and usually wins.

Life gives no one immunity against adversity, but life gives to everyone the power of positive thought, which is sufficient to master all circumstances of adversity and convert them into benefits. The individual is left with the privilege of using or neglecting to use his prerogative right to think his way through all adversities. Every individual is forced either to use his thought power for the attainment of definite, positive ends, or by neglect or design use this power for the attainment of negative ends. There can be no compromise, no refusal to use the mind.

The law of hypnotic rhythm forces every individual to give some degree of use, either negative or positive, to his mind, but it does not influence the individual as to which use he will make of his mind.

Q. Am I to understand from what you say that every adversity is a blessing?

A. No, I did not say that. I said there is the seed of an equivalent advantage in every adversity. I did not say there was the full-blown flower of advantage, just the seed. Usually the seed consists of some form of knowledge, some idea or plan, or some opportunity which would not have been available except through the change of thought-habits forced by the adversity.

Q. Are those all the benefits available to human beings through failure?

A. No, failure is used by nature as a common language in which she chastises people when they neglect to adapt themselves to her laws.

For example, the world war was man-made and destructive. Nature planted in the circumstances of the war the seed of an equivalent reprimand in the form of a world depression. The depression was inevitable and inescapable. It followed the war as naturally as day follows night and by the operation of the self-same law, the law of hypnotic rhythm.

Q. Am I to understand that the law of hypnotic rhythm is the same as that which Ralph Waldo Emerson called the law of compensation?

A. The law of hypnotic rhythm is the law of compensation. It is the power with which nature balances negative and positive forces throughout the universes, in all forms of energy, in all forms of matter, and in all human relationships.

Q. Does the law of hypnotic rhythm operate quickly in all instances? For example, does this law immediately bless one with the benefits of positive application of thoughts, or curse one immediately with the results of negative thoughts?

A. The law operates definitely but not always swiftly. Both the benefits and the penalties incurred through the law by individuals may be harvested by others, either before or after their death.

Observe how this law works by forcing upon one generation of people the effects of both the sins and the virtues of preceding generations. In the operation of all of nature's laws, the fourth dimension, time, is an inexorable factor. The length of time consumed by nature in the relation of effects to their causes depends, in every instance, on the circumstances at hand.

Nature grows a pumpkin in three months. A good size oak tree requires a hundred years. She converts a hen's egg into a chicken in four weeks, but she requires nine months to convert the egg of a human being into an individual.

STUDY GUIDE

Chapter 11:
Learning from Adversity

1. The dialogue opens with a conversation around the benefits of failure. The Devil clarifies that he takes over individuals after they quit trying. Have you experienced a form of so-called failure in your life, where, in retrospect, you think you could have been successful if you hadn't given up? If you have, please write about your experience.

2. The Devil also stated that all forms of defeat and failure bring people the seed of unborn opportunity because it often breaks the grip of hypnotic rhythm. Have you (or someone you know) experienced a situation in your life when you/they became lethargic or complacent when working toward a goal, only to find that apparent failure snapped you/them out of that state and into final success? Please describe such a situation.

3. Napoleon Hill shares the revelation that "the law of hypnotic rhythm is capable of both negative and positive application. It may drag one down to slavery through loss of the privilege of freedom of thought, or it may help one rise to great heights of achievement through the free use of thought, depending on how the individual relates himself to the law." Do you believe you tend toward negativity or positivity when you have related to this law previously in your life?

4. The Devil claims that failure is a man-made circumstance—that it is a state of mind in which one has the privilege of clearing fear and starting in a new direction. Write about at least two experiences where you found yourself overwhelmed with fear—circumstances you were able to clear from your mind and move beyond. They could be as simple as overcoming fear of the dark as a child, to fear of driving, or fear of going back to work after being fired.

5. The Devil also states that fear gives you an opportunity to test yourself so that ultimately you can learn how powerful you are. On a scale

from 1 to 10 (1 being "very little" and 10 being "very much so"), rate how powerful you believe yourself to be:

1 —— 2 —— 3 —— 4 —— 5 —— 6 —— 7 —— 8 —— 9 —— 10

6. Now on a scale from 1 to 10 (1 being "very little" and 10 being "very much so"), rate how powerful you believe you potentially could be:

1 —— 2 —— 3 —— 4 —— 5 —— 6 —— 7 —— 8 —— 9 —— 10

7. Failure can also help you to learn truths about yourself and the world. Focus on a particular situation in which you experienced apparent failure. What did you learn from the experience? If your first thought is that you learned nothing, continue to earnestly search and ask your subconscious to reveal any truths that your consciousness has been avoiding.

8. Do research on someone who you believed to be revolutionary and highly successful. Focus specifically on the apparent failures they experienced, and the times that others told them to give up their quest. Do you believe that you, too, could experience such perseverance? Why or why not?

9. What self-talk message(s) would you have to change within your own mind to gain more perseverance when focusing on your life goals?

10. The Devil states that the only permanent thing in the universe is change, as is evident in nature: "She uses economic depressions to break the rhythm of mass thought when great numbers of people become improperly related—through business, social, and political activities." Give at least one example of this in the history of the world (other than the 1929 Depression).

11. The Devil goes on to assert that what we call "character" is nothing more than a manifestation of the law of hypnotic rhythm—one's thought habits that have been crystallized into either a positive or negative personality. Focus on two individuals that you know—one whom you respect, and the other whom you do not. Do you believe their main thought patterns influenced the person they have become? Please explain.

12. Proper marital relationship begins with a proper motive for the relationship. If you are married (or have been in the past), write what you believed your most prominent motive to be.

13. Reflecting on the relationship, were your words and actions mostly positive and uplifting or negative?

14. Reflect on a relationship in which you were involved that you believe failed. Usually both parties are responsible for its success or failure. Did you engage in negative dialogue and behaviors?

15. If you didn't see yourself as speaking or acting negatively, were your thoughts about the relationship or the other individual negative in nature? Please explain.

16. Similarly, consider a relationship in which you are or were involved that is very positive in nature. What thoughts, words, and deeds did you add to the experience?

17. Describe a situation in which you were able to pivot your habits to focus less on what you don't want, and more on what you do want. If you can't think of one, then commit to creating one within the next two weeks.

18. Do you believe you have successfully changed yourself throughout your life? How have you done so?

19. The Devil states that the subconscious mind of man "consists of universal energy (Infinite Intelligence) which each person receives, appropriates and organizes into definite thought forms." Do you believe this to be true? Why or why not?

20. Emotion-laden thoughts can wreak havoc in individuals who do not exercise self-discipline and can often cause relational disharmony. Reflect on your life. When has there been a situation in which you passionately blurted out a response without giving adequate consideration prior? Did you later regret your reactiveness? Why or why not?

21. The Devil states that one can receive organized thoughts of others through their sixth sense. Do you believe you have a strong sixth sense? Do you have proof of your opinion on this? Please provide it.

22. Proper relationship is defined as one that "brings all connected with it, or affected by it, some form of benefit." The opposite, improper relationship "damages anyone or brings any form of misery or unhappiness to any of the individuals." List at least two people with whom you believe you have "proper relationship." Now list two individuals with whom you have or have had "improper relationship." What role have you played in each relationship (in other words, what do you own responsibility for in the relationship)?

23. Do you believe that the adversities you have faced in your life have helped you to become more mindful, introspective, and honest with

yourself? If so, what have you learned about yourself? Did you make any behavioral changes in response to the insights you gained? Please explain.

24. Did adversity draw you to seek intelligence from sources beyond your own mind? If so, what new conclusions did you come to?

25. Were you able to break any old thought habits in response to adversities in your life? Take some time to reflect on the adversities you have faced, and the changes you made in response to them.

26. Has failure ever opened you up to depend more upon spiritual forces? If so, how?

27. Have you ever lost money or material things? If so, did you become acutely aware of the impermanence of life?

28. What do you understand the law of compensation to be?

29. The Devil suggests that you can see the law of compensation at work through the observation of generations of people in response to the effects of both the sins and virtues of their ancestors. Research a culture in which this principle has been revealed in history and write about it.

Chapter 12

Environment, Time, Harmony and Caution

Q I now have a better understanding of the potentialities of adversity and failure. You may go ahead, now, with your description of the next of the seven principles. What is your next principle?

A. The next principle is *environmental influence.*

Q Go ahead and describe the working principle of environmental influences as a determining factor in human destinies.

A. Environment consists of all the mental, spiritual, and physical forces which affect and influence human beings.

Q What connection, if any, is there between environmental influences and hypnotic rhythm?

A. Hypnotic rhythm solidifies and makes permanent the thought-habits of human beings. Thought-habits are stimulated by environmental influences. In other words, the material on which thoughts are fed comes from one's environment. Thought-habits are made permanent by hypnotic rhythm.

Q What is the most important part of one's environment, the part which determines, more than all others, whether an individual makes positive or negative use of his mind?
A. The most important part of one's environment is that created by his association with others. All people absorb and take over, either consciously or unconsciously, the thought-habits of those with whom they associate closely.

Q Do you mean by this that constant association with a person whose thought-habits are negative influences one to form negative thought-habits?
A. Yes, the law of hypnotic rhythm forces every human being to form thought-habits which harmonize with the dominating influences of his environment, particularly that part of his environment created by his association with other minds.

Q Then it is important that one select one's close associates with great care?
A. Yes, one's intimate associates should be chosen with as much care as one chooses the food with which he feeds his body, with the object always of associating with people whose dominating thoughts are positive, friendly, and harmonious.

Q Which class of associates has the greatest influence upon one?
A. One's partner in marriage and in the home and one's associates in his occupation. After that come close friends and acquaintances. Casual acquaintances and strangers have but little influence on one.

Q Why does one's partner in marriage have so great an influence upon one's mind?
A. Because the relationship of marriage brings people under the influence of spiritual forces of such weight that they become dominating forces of the mind.

Q How may environmental influences be used to break the grip of hypnotic rhythm?

A. All influences which establish thought-habits are given permanency through the law of hypnotic rhythm. One may change the influences of his environment so that the dominating influences are either positive or negative, and the law of hypnotic rhythm will make them permanent, unless they are changed through one's habits of thought.

Q Stating this truth in another way, one may submit himself to any environmental influence desired, whether positive or negative, and the law of hypnotic rhythm will make the influence permanent when it assumes the magnitude of thought habit. Is that the way the law works?

A. That is correct. Be careful of all forces which inspire thought; those are the forces which constitute environment and determine the nature of one's earthly destiny.

Q What class of people controls their environmental influences?

A. The non-drifters. All who are victims of the habit of drifting forfeit their power to choose their own environment. They become the victims of every negative influence of their environment.

Q Is there no way out for the drifter? Is there no method by which he may submit himself to the influence of a positive environment?

A. Yes, there is a way out for drifters. They can stop drifting, take possession of their own minds, and choose an environment which inspires positive thought. This they may accomplish through definiteness of purpose.

Q Is that all there is to the act of eliminating the habit of drifting? Is the habit only a state of mind?

A. Drifting is nothing but a negative state of mind, a state of mind conspicuous by its emptiness of purpose.

Q What effective procedure may one follow in establishing an environment most helpful in developing and maintaining positive thought-habits?

A. The most effective of all environments is that which may be created by a friendly alliance of a group of people who will obligate themselves to assist one another in achieving the object of some definite purpose. This sort of an alliance is known as a Master Mind. Through its operation one may associate himself with carefully chosen individuals each of whom brings to the alliance some knowledge, experience, education, plan, or idea suited to his needs in carrying out the object of his definite purpose.

The most successful leaders in all walks of life avail themselves of this sort of made-to-order environmental influence. Outstanding achievement is impossible without the friendly cooperation of others. Stating the truth in another way, successful people must control their environment, thereby insuring themselves against the influence of a negative environment.

Q What of people whose duty to relatives makes it impossible for them to avoid the influence of a negative environment?

A. No human being owes another any degree of duty which robs him of his privilege of building his thought-habits in a positive environment. On the other hand, every human being is duty bound to himself to remove from his environment every influence which even remotely tends to develop negative thought-habits.

Q Isn't this a cold-blooded philosophy?

A. Only the strong survive. No one can be strong without removing himself from all influences which develop negative thought-habits. Negative thought-habits result in the loss of the privilege of self-determination, no matter what or who may cause those habits. Positive thought-habits may be controlled by the individual and made to serve his aims and purposes. Negative thought-habits control the individual and deprive him of the privilege of self-determination.

Q I deduce from all you have said that those who control the environmental influences out of which their thought habits are built are masters of their earthly destinies and that all others are mastered by earthly destinies. Is that stating the matter correctly?

A. Perfectly stated.

Q What establishes one's thought-habits?

A. All habits are established because of inherent or acquired desires, or motives. That is, habits are begun as the result of some form of definite desire.

Q What takes place in the physical brain while one is forming thought-habits?

A. Desires are organized impulses of energy called thoughts. Desires that are mixed with emotional feeling magnetize the brain cells in which they are stored and prepare those cells to be taken over and directed by the law of hypnotic rhythm. When any thought appears in the brain or is created there, and is mixed with keen emotional feeling of desire, the law of hypnotic rhythm begins, at once, to translate it into its physical counterpart.

Dominating thoughts, which are acted upon first by the law of hypnotic rhythm, are those with which are mixed the strongest desires and the most intense feelings. Thought habits are established by the repetition of the same thoughts.

Q What are the most impelling basic motives or desires which inspire thought action?

A. The ten most common motives, those which inspire most of one's thought-action, are these:
- The desire for sex expression and love
- The desire for physical food
- The desire for spiritual, mental, and physical self-expression
- The desire for perpetuation of life after death
- The desire for power over others

- The desire for material wealth
- The desire for knowledge
- The desire to imitate others
- The desire to excel others
- The seven basic fears

These are the dominating motives which inspire the majority of all human endeavors.

Q What about the negative desires such as greed, envy, avarice, jealousy, anger? Are these not expressed more often than any of the positive desires?

A. All negative desires are nothing but frustrations of positive desires.

They are inspired by some form of defeat, failure, or neglect by human beings to adapt themselves to nature's laws in a positive way.

Q That's a new slant on the subject of negative thoughts. If I correctly understand what you have said, all negative thoughts are inspired by one's neglect or failure to adapt oneself harmoniously to nature's laws. Is that correct?

A. That is exactly correct. Nature will not tolerate idleness or vacuums of any sort. All space must be and is filled with something.

Everything in existence, of both a physical and a spiritual nature, must be and is constantly in motion. The human brain is no exception. It was created to receive, organize, specialize, and express the power of thought. When the individual does not use the brain for the expression of positive, creative thoughts, nature fills the vacuum by forcing the brain to act upon negative thoughts.

There can be no idleness in the brain. Understand this principle and you will come into a new and important understanding of the part environmental influences take in the lives of human beings.

You will better understand, also, how the law of hypnotic rhythm operates, it being the law which keeps everything and everyone constantly moving through some form of expression of either negative or positive principles.

Nature is not interested in morals as such. She is not interested in right and wrong. She is not interested in justice and injustice. She is interested only in forcing everything to express action according to its nature!

Q That is an enlightening interpretation of nature's ways. To whom may I turn for corroboration of your claims?

A. To men of science, to the philosophers, to all accurate thinkers.

Lastly, to the physical manifestations of nature herself.

Nature has no such thing as dead matter. Every atom of matter is constantly in a state of motion. All energy is constantly in motion. There are no dead voids anywhere. Time and space are literally manifestations of motion of such swiftness that it cannot be measured by human beings.

Q Alas, one is forced to the conclusion, from what you say, that the sources of dependable knowledge are shockingly limited.

A. The developed sources of knowledge are limited. Every normal adult human brain is a potential gateway to all the knowledge there is throughout the universes. Every normal adult brain has within its mechanism the possibility of direct communication with Infinite Intelligence, wherein exists all the knowledge that is or can ever be.

Q Your statement leads me to believe that human beings may become all they have attributed to what they call God. Is that what you mean?

A. Through the law of evolution the human brain is being perfected to communicate at will with Infinite Intelligence. The perfection will come through organized development of the brain, through its adaptation to nature's laws. Time is the factor which will bring perfection.

Q. What causes cycles of recurring events, such as epidemics of disease, business depressions, wars, and crime waves?

A. All such epidemics in which great numbers of people are similarly affected are caused by the law of hypnotic rhythm, through which nature consolidates thoughts of a similar nature and causes those thoughts to be expressed through mass action.

Q. Then the Great Depression was put into motion because great numbers of people were influenced to release thoughts of fear. Is that correct?

A. Perfectly. Millions of people were endeavoring to get something for nothing, through stock gambling. When they suddenly discovered they had gotten nothing for something, they became frightened, rushed to their banks to draw out their balances, and the panic was on. Through mass thought of millions of minds, all thinking in terms of fear of poverty, the depression was prolonged over a period of years.

Q. From what you say, I deduce that nature consolidates the dominating thoughts of people and expresses these thoughts through some form of mass action, such as business depressions, business booms, and so on. Is that correct?

A. You have the right idea.

Q. Let us now take up the next of the seven principles. Go ahead and describe it.

A. The next principle is *time*, the fourth dimension.

Q. What relationship is there between time and the operation of the law of hypnotic rhythm?

A. Time is the law of hypnotic rhythm. The lapse of time required to give permanency to thought-habits depends upon the object and the nature of the thoughts.

Q But I understood you to say that the only enduring thing in nature is change. If that is true, then time is constantly changing, rearranging, and recombining all things, including one's thought-habits. How, then, could the law of hypnotic rhythm give permanency to one's thought-habits?

A. Time divides all thought-habits into two classes, negative thoughts and positive thoughts. One's individual thoughts are of course constantly changing and being recombined to suit the individual's desires, but thoughts do not change from negative to positive or vice versa except through voluntary effort on the part of the individual.

Time penalizes the individual for all negative thoughts and rewards him for all positive thoughts, according to the nature and purpose of the thoughts. If one's dominating thoughts are negative, time penalizes the individual by building in his mind the habit of negative thinking and then proceeds to solidify this habit into permanency every second of its existence. Positive thoughts are, likewise, woven by time into permanent habits. The term "permanency," of course, refers to the natural life of the individual. In the strict sense of the term, nothing is permanent. Time converts thought-habits into what might be called permanency during the life of the individual.

Q Now I have a better understanding of how time works. What other characteristics has time in connection with the earthly destiny of human beings?

A. Time is nature's seasoning influence through which human experience may be ripened into wisdom. People are not born with wisdom, but they are born with the capacity to think, and they may, through the lapse of time, think their way into wisdom.

Q Do youths ever possess wisdom?

A. Only in very elementary matters. Wisdom comes only through the lapse of time. It cannot be inherited and it cannot be imparted from one person to another except through the lapse of time.

Q Does the lapse of time force an individual to acquire wisdom?
A. No! Wisdom comes only to non-drifters who form positive thought-habits as a dominating force in their lives. Drifters and those whose dominating thoughts are negative never acquire wisdom except of a very elementary nature.

Q From what you say, I infer that time is the friend of the person who trains his mind to follow positive thought-habits and the enemy of the person who drifts into negative thought-habits. Is that correct?
A. That is precisely true. All people can be classified as drifters and non-drifters. Drifters are always at the mercy of the non-drifters, and time makes this relationship permanent.

Q Do you mean that if I drift along through life, without definite aim or purpose, the non-drifter may become my master, and time only serves to give the non-drifter a stronger and more permanent grip upon me?
A. That is stating the truth exactly.

Q What is wisdom?
A. Wisdom is the ability to relate yourself to nature's laws so as to make them serve you, and the ability to relate yourself to other people so as to gain their harmonious, willing cooperation in helping you to make life yield whatever you demand of it.

Q Then accumulated knowledge is not wisdom?
A. Great heavens, no! If knowledge were wisdom, the achievements of science would not have been converted into implements of destruction.

Q What is needed to convert knowledge into wisdom?
A. Time plus the desire for wisdom. Wisdom is never thrust upon one. It is acquired, if at all, by positive thinking, through voluntary effort!

Q Is it safe for all people to have knowledge?

A. It is never safe for anyone to have extensive knowledge without wisdom.

Q What is the age at which most people who acquire wisdom begin to acquire it?

A. The majority of people who acquire wisdom do so after they have passed the age of forty. Prior to that time the majority of people are too busy gathering knowledge and organizing it into plans to spend any effort seeking wisdom.

Q What circumstance of life is most apt to lead one to acquire wisdom?

A. Adversity and failure. These are nature's universal languages through which she imparts wisdom to those who are ready to receive it.

Q Do adversity and failure always bring wisdom?

A. No, only to those who are ready for wisdom and have voluntarily sought it.

Q What determines one's readiness to receive wisdom?

A. Time and the nature of one's thought-habits.

Q Is newly acquired knowledge the same as time-tested knowledge?

A. No, knowledge tested through the lapse of time always is superior to that which has been newly acquired. Time gives to knowledge definiteness in both quality and quantity, and dependability. One never can be sure of knowledge that has not been tested.

Q What is dependable knowledge?

A. It is knowledge which harmonizes with natural law, which means that it is based upon positive thought.

Q Does time modify and alter the values of knowledge?
A. Yes, time modifies and alters all values. That which is accurate knowledge today may become null and void tomorrow because of time's rearrangement of facts and values. Time modifies all human relationships for better or for worse, depending upon the policy through which people relate themselves to one another.

In the realm of thought there is a time when it is proper to sow the seeds of thought, and there is a proper time to reap the harvest of those thoughts, the same as there is a time to sow and a time to reap from the soil of the earth. Without the proper measurement of time between the sowing and the reaping, nature modifies or withholds the rewards of the sowing.

Q Go ahead, now, and describe the last two of the seven principles.
A. The next principle is *harmony*.

Throughout nature one may find evidences that all natural law moves in an orderly manner, through the law of harmony. Through the operation of this law nature forces everything within the range of a given environment to become harmoniously related. Understand this truth and you will catch a new and a more intriguing vision of the power of environment. You will understand why association with negative minds is fatal to those seeking self-determination.

Q Do you mean that nature voluntarily forces human beings to harmonize with the influences of their environment?
A. Yes, that is true. The law of hypnotic rhythm forces upon every living thing the dominating influences of the environment in which it exists.

Q If nature forces human beings to take on the nature of the environment in which they live, what means of escape are available to people who find themselves in an environment of poverty and failure but desire to escape?

A. They must change their environment or remain poverty-stricken.

Nature permits no one to escape the influences of his environment.

However, nature, in her abundance of wisdom, has given to every normal human being the privilege of establishing his own mental, spiritual, and physical environment, but once he establishes it he must become a part of it. This is the inexorable working of the law of harmony.

Q. In a business association, for example, who establishes the dominating influence that determines the rhythm of the environment?

A. The individual or individuals who think and act with definiteness of purpose.

Q. Is it as simple as that?

A. Yes, definiteness of purpose is the starting point from which an individual may establish his own environment.

Q. I do not seem to follow your reasoning. The entire world is torn with warfare and business depressions and other forms of strife which represent about everything except harmony. Nature does not seem to be forcing people to harmonize with one another. How do you explain this inconsistency?

A. There is no inconsistency. The dominating influences of the world are, as you say, negative. Very well, nature is forcing human beings to harmonize with the dominating influences of the world environment.

Manifestations of harmony may be either positive or negative. For example, a group of men in prison may, and they generally do, think and act in a negative manner, but nature sees to it that the dominating influence of the prison is impressed upon every individual in it. A group of poverty-stricken people in a tenement house may fight among themselves and apparently resist all forms of harmony, but nature forces each of them to become a part of the dominating influence of the house in which they live.

Harmony, in the sense it is here used, means that nature relates everything throughout the universes to every other thing of a similar nature. Negative influences are forced into association with one another, no matter where they may be. Positive influences are just as definitely forced into association with one another.

Q I am beginning to see why successful business leaders are so careful in the choice of their business associates. Men who succeed in any calling usually establish their own environment by surrounding themselves with people who think and act in terms of success. Is that the idea?

A. That is the idea exactly. Observe, with profit, that the one thing all successful men insist upon is harmony among their business associates.

Another trait of successful people is that they move with definiteness of purpose and insist upon their associates doing the same. Understand these two truths and you understand the major difference between a Henry Ford and a day laborer.

Q Now tell me about the last of the seven principles.

A. The last principle is *caution*.

Next to the habit of drifting, the most dangerous human trait is the lack of caution.

People drift into all sorts of hazardous circumstances because they do not exercise caution by planning the moves they make. The drifter always moves without exercising caution. He acts first and thinks later, if at all. He does not choose his friends. He drifts along and allows people to attach themselves to him on their own terms. He does not choose an occupation. He drifts through school and is glad to get the first job that will give him food and clothing. He invites people to cheat him at trade by neglecting to inform himself of the rules of trade. He invites illness by neglecting to inform himself of the rules of sound health. He invites poverty by neglecting to protect himself against the environmental influences of the poverty-stricken. He invites failure at every step he takes by neglecting to exercise the caution to observe what causes people to fail. He invites fear in all its forms by his lack of caution in examining the causes of fear. He fails in marriage because he neglects to use caution in his choice of a mate, and he uses still less caution in his methods of relating himself to her after marriage. He loses his friends or converts them into enemies by his lack of caution in relating himself to them on the proper basis.

Q Are all people lacking in caution?
A. No, only those who have acquired the habit of drifting. The non-drifter always uses caution. He carefully thinks his plans through before he begins them. He makes allowances for the human frailties of his associates and plans ahead to bridge them.

If he sends a messenger on an important mission, he sends someone else to make sure the messenger does not neglect his mission. Then he checks on both of them to be sure his wishes have been fulfilled. He takes nothing for granted where caution provides a way to insure his success.

Q Isn't over-caution as detrimental as lack of caution?
A. There is no such thing as over-caution. What you call "over caution" is an expression of fear. Fear and caution are two entirely different things.

Q Don't people mistake fear for over-caution?
A. Yes, that does sometimes happen, but the majority of people create for themselves far more disastrous hazards by total lack of the habit of caution than by over-caution.

Q In what way may caution be used most advantageously?
A. In the selection of one's associates and in one's method of relating oneself to associates. The reason for this is obvious.

One's associates constitute the most important part of one's environment, and environmental influences determine whether one forms the habit of drifting or becomes a non-drifter. The person who exercises due caution in the choice of associates never allows himself to be closely associated with any person who does not bring to him, through the association, some definite mental, spiritual, or economic benefit.

Q Isn't that method of choosing associates selfish?
A. It is sensible and leads to self-determination. It is the desire of every normal person to find material success and happiness.

Nothing contributes more to one's success and happiness than carefully chosen associates. Caution in the selection of associates becomes, therefore, the duty of every person who wishes to become happy and successful. The drifter allows his closest associates to attach themselves to him on their own terms. The non-drifter carefully selects his associates and allows no one to become closely associated with him unless that person contributes some form of helpful influence or bestows some definite benefit.

Q It never occurred to me that caution in the selection of friends had so definite a bearing on one's success or failure. Do all successful people exercise caution in the selection of all their associates, whether in business, social, or professional relationships?
A. Without the exercise of caution in the choice of all associates, no one may be certain of success in any calling. On the other hand, lack of exercise of caution brings almost certain defeat in whatever one undertakes.

STUDY GUIDE

Chapter 12:
Environment, Time, Harmony, and Caution

1. The next principle discussed is environmental influence. Environment is defined as "all mental, spiritual, and physical forces which affect and influence human beings." How much do you believe your environment affects you over your DNA?

2. According to this conversation, your environment is most shaped by those with whom you associate in your life. Make a list of your three closest family members, three personal friends, and three of your closest business associates. Reflect on each to ascertain whether they are primarily positive or negative influences.

3. Are there areas of your environment that you should change to avoid hypnotic rhythm that may not be healthy? On a scale from 1 to 10 (1 being "very little" and 10 being "very much so"), rate the health of each of the following environments in your life.

    Home/Marriage:
    1 — 2 — 3 — 4 — 5 — 6 — 7 — 8 — 9 — 10

    Employment:
    1 — 2 — 3 — 4 — 5 — 6 — 7 — 8 — 9 — 10

    Friendships:
    1 — 2 — 3 — 4 — 5 — 6 — 7 — 8 — 9 — 10

    Community (school, church, social organizations, for example):
    1 — 2 — 3 — 4 — 5 — 6 — 7 — 8 — 9 — 10

4. Which of the above areas of your life can you take immediate action to improve? How are you planning to do so?

5. Do you believe that you have control over your environmental influences? Why or why not? Please explain.

6. What new environment could you introduce yourself to that would inspire greater positive thought habits?

7. Plan to take the first step toward integrating the new, healthier environment into your life. Set up action steps and projected completion dates for this task. Be sure to see yourself experiencing it effortlessly, with great joy and enthusiasm. Then take the first step, no matter how small it may be.

8. The most effective environment is one that is within a friendly alliance via a group who obligate themselves to assist one another in achieving the objects of their desire/definite purpose. A masterminding group, Toastmasters, your community chamber of commerce, Habitat for Humanity, and other such structured organizations can assist you with this. Do you belong to any such groups? If not, do you have an interest in joining one. If so, take an action step toward doing so.

9. The Devil stated, "Outstanding achievement is impossible without the friendly cooperation of others." List at least three new people in various environments in your life that you believe would be supportive and a positive influence on you. Then make a commitment to getting to know them and adding them to your sphere of influence.

10. Are there any negative environments in which you are currently exposed to that you should consider leaving? If so, list them and, if possible, take some action steps toward doing so.

11. Are there any negative people currently in your life from whom you should consider distancing yourself? If so, list them and, if possible, take some action steps toward doing so.

12. Gossip is a toxic and negative habit. Do you currently use gossip as a means of connecting with your family members, friends, or colleagues? If so, congratulations for owning this toxic habit. Now that you are aware of it, do you think you can commit to avoiding bad-mouthing others?

13. Your thought habits are established by your inherent or acquired desires or motives. What is the strongest desire that you currently have in your life?

14. Do you see how that desire shapes your thought habits? Please explain.

15. The ten most common motives that inspire most of one's thought-action are listed below. Reflect on each and on a scale from 1 to 10

(1 being "very little" and 10 being "very much so"), rate the degree to which you desire them.

1 — 2 — 3 — 4 — 5 — 6 — 7 — 8 — 9 — 10

The desire for sex expression and love:

1 — 2 — 3 — 4 — 5 — 6 — 7 — 8 — 9 — 10

The desire for physical food:

1 — 2 — 3 — 4 — 5 — 6 — 7 — 8 — 9 — 10

The desire for spiritual, mental, and physical self-expression:

1 — 2 — 3 — 4 — 5 — 6 — 7 — 8 — 9 — 10

The desire for perpetuation of life after death:

1 — 2 — 3 — 4 — 5 — 6 — 7 — 8 — 9 — 10

The desire for power over others:

1 — 2 — 3 — 4 — 5 — 6 — 7 — 8 — 9 — 10

The desire for material wealth:

1 — 2 — 3 — 4 — 5 — 6 — 7 — 8 — 9 — 10

The desire for knowledge:

1 — 2 — 3 — 4 — 5 — 6 — 7 — 8 — 9 — 10

The desire to imitate others:

1 — 2 — 3 — 4 — 5 — 6 — 7 — 8 — 9 — 10

The desire to excel over others:

1 — 2 — 3 — 4 — 5 — 6 — 7 — 8 — 9 — 10

The seven basic fears:

1 — 2 — 3 — 4 — 5 — 6 — 7 — 8 — 9 — 10

16. It is stated that nature will not tolerate idleness or energetic vacuums. Are there areas of your life in which you are idle, or where you perceive there are energetic vacuums? If so, please list them.

17. It was stated that nature is not interested in right or wrong, justice or injustice. If this is the case, then any moral judgment you have works against nature. What can you conclude about this insight regarding your life? Does this realization change your perception in any way? If so, please explain.

18. If all is action- and motion-oriented, are there any areas in your life in which you think more "motion" would be beneficial to you? If so, where?

19. It is said that human beings may become all that has been attributed to what is called "God"—that you can be perfected to communicate at will with Infinite Intelligence. How do you feel about this statement?

20. It is said that all epidemics are caused by the low of hypnotic rhythm through mass action. Reflecting on the COVID epidemic, if this is the case, how do you believe it was manifested on earth?

21. If nature consolidates the Dominating Thoughts of people and expresses them through mass action, then what do you believe are the current Dominating Thoughts of people on this earth? How do you believe these can manifest? In what way?

22. The next principle is time, the fourth dimension. It is said that time penalizes negative thoughts and rewards all positive thoughts. Thus, if you are a negative thinker, in time, negative thoughts will build a permanence in your life. List at least one recurring negative thought that you would like to shift to a positive one. Once you have done so, make a commitment to changing it. Then track your success.

23. Wisdom is defined as "the ability to relate yourself to nature's laws so as to make them serve you." In what areas of your life do you believe you have developed wisdom? If wisdom comes only through a lapse of time, do you believe that time played a role in their development?

24. You must have a desire for wisdom to achieve it, and knowledge without wisdom is not safe. Are there areas in your life where you believe you have acquired knowledge, but not yet wisdom? If so, do you have a burning desire to transmute that knowledge into wisdom?

25. Wisdom is acquired alongside time through adversity and failure. Do you believe you have lived long enough on this earth and experienced enough adversity and failure to become an extremely wise person? Is this important to you? Why or why not?

26. Wisdom can be voluntarily sought. There are many people who can voluntarily learn from the mistakes of others, while some must experience those mistakes themselves before learning. Which are you?

27. The next principle is harmony. It is said that nature voluntarily forces human beings to harmonize with the influences of their environment. With this truth, the power of the media comes to mind. If you constantly bombard yourself with negative and fear-based messaging

from the media, then do you believe you will start to harmonize with them? If so, is there a way that you can minimize or shield yourself from negative messaging? If so, how?

28. If this is the case, if you are living in poverty and harmonizing with poverty-consciousness, then do you believe you can shift these influences through creative visualization and appreciating along with imaging the abundance that you desire in your life? If so, then take at least five minutes to visualize the abundance that you seek.

29. It is stated that one thing all successful businessmen and businesswomen insist upon is harmony, and definiteness of purpose among their associates. Do you see evidence of this in your workplace? Are there ways in which it could be improved? If so, then list them.

30. The last of the seven principles is caution. Second to drifting, lack of caution is the most dangerous human trait. Are there areas of your life where you think you have drifted into circumstances that do not support your personal growth and success? If so, then list them.

31. List the ways in which you exercise caution in your life to ensure success.

32. You need to exercise caution most with the associates that you choose in your life. You should only associate with individuals who bring you "some definite mental, spiritual or economic benefit." Go back to the list you previously created of family, friends, and business associates at the beginning of this chapter. Review each individual and assess whether you believe each brings you mental, spiritual, or economic benefits.

33. The three things that Napoleon Hill connected most with in his interview with the Devil were (1) The habit of drifting, (2) The low of hypnotic rhythm, and (3) the element of time. Reflecting on the contents of this book thus far, list the elements that have most impacted you.

34. Napoleon Hill challenges you to "take any circumstance you wish, measure it with reference to its relationship to the habit of drifting, hypnotic rhythm, and time, and you may ascertain accurately the cause of all success and all failure." Reflect on at least one such circumstance and list the ways in which these three elements affected the outcome.

35. Franklin D. Roosevelt is cited as an example of shifting fear among the American masses to faith. Reflecting on history, write about at least one other influential individual who was able to make such a shift.

36. Is there anyone in your life that you believe can shift masses of negativity into positivity? If so, please describe them.

37. Napoleon Hill stated that Roosevelt was a prime example of moving from definiteness of purpose into drifting. Can you think of anyone in your life or in the public world who has followed a similar path? If so, what was their ultimate demise?

38. The author believed that many marriages that he researched failed because of accumulated small incidents that weakened the fiber of the marriage due to a lack of definiteness of purpose. Does your primary relationship have a definite purpose (if you are not in a relationship, note your own relationship with yourself)? If not, take some time to write one down.

39. The brief sentence that Napoleon Hill writes that encapsulates the overriding message of the book is, "One's dominating desires can be crystallized into their physical equivalents through definiteness of purpose backed by definiteness of plans, with the aid of nature's law of hypnotic rhythm and time!" Based on your own self-inquiry and reflection, would you add any additional insights to this sentence?

40. Napoleon Hill ultimately learned that success and failure are the results of day-to-day evolutionary forces that are pieced together through our Dominating Thoughts and woven into the things that we want and don't want. He said that he could have saved himself a great deal of difficulty had he seen this prior. Do you believe that by reading this book, and completing the exercises, you have prevented some further potential difficulties in your life? Please explain.

41. Napoleon Hill states that you need to agree with every portion of his interview with the Devil to benefit from it. Are there any insights shared that you struggled with? If so, write them down and then reread the book to seek answers.

42. Before concluding this chapter, write a list of action steps you are committing to take to shift your life into more definiteness of purpose. When possible, list timelines for when you plan on making the shifts and hold to those commitments, knowing that focus, purpose, and time are all assisting you with manifesting all that you truly desire.

Summary

Three things connected with my interview with the Devil interest me most. These three factors interest me because they have been the most important influences in my own life, a fact which any reader of my story can easily discern. The three important factors are the habit of drifting, the law of hypnotic rhythm through which all habits are made permanent, and the element of time.

Here is a trio of forces which hold inviolate the destinies of all men. The three take on a new and more important meaning when they are grouped and studied as a combined force. It takes but little imagination and scarcely any understanding of natural laws for one to see that most of the difficulties in which people find themselves are of their own making. Moreover, difficulties seldom are the outgrowth of immediate circumstances. They are generally the climax of a series of circumstances which have been consolidated through the habit of drifting and with the aid of time.

Samuel Insull did not lose his $4 billion industrial empire as the result of the depression. He began losing it long before the depression when he became the victim of a group of women who flattered him into turning his talents from public utilities to grand opera. If ever a man in a high position in the financial world went down because of the power of drifting, hypnotic rhythm, and time, that man was Samuel Insull. I am writing from accurate knowledge of Mr. Insull and the cause of his troubles dating from the time that I served with him during the World War to the time of his ill-advised attempt to run away from himself.

Henry Ford went through the same depression that swept Mr. Insull under, but Ford came out on top without a scratch. Do you want to know the reason? I'll tell you. Ford has the habit of not drifting on any subject. Time is Ford's friend because he has formed the habit of using it in a positive, constructive manner, with the aid of thoughts of his own making, woven into plans of his own creation.

Take any circumstance you wish, measure it with reference to its relationship to the habit of drifting, hypnotic rhythm, and time, and you may ascertain accurately the cause of all success and all failure.

Franklin D. Roosevelt went into office with a bang during his first term. He had but one major purpose in mind and that was very definite. It was to stop the stampede of fear and start people to thinking and talking in terms of business recovery instead of business depression.

In carrying out that purpose, there was no drifting. The forces of the entire nation were consolidated and moved as one to help carry out the President's definite purpose. For the first time in the history of America, the newspapers of all political leanings, the churches of all denominations, the people of all races and colors, and the political organizations of all brands united themselves into one stupendous power for the sole purpose of helping the President restore faith and normal business relationships in the country.

In a conference held between the President and a group of emergency advisers a few days after he went into office, I asked him what was his major problem. He replied, "It is not a question of majors and minors; we have but one problem and that is to stop fear and supplant it with faith."

Before the end of his first year in office, the President had stopped fear and supplanted it by faith, and the nation was slowly but surely on the way out of the jungle of depression. By the end of his first term—mark well the element of lapse of time—the President had so effectively consolidated the forces of American business and private life that he had an entire nation in back of him, ready, willing, and enthusiastically desirous of following his lead no matter which way he went.

These are facts well known to everyone who reads newspapers or listens to the radio.

Then came another presidential election and the opportunity for the people to express their faith in their leader. They expressed it in a landslide without precedent in American politics, and the President went into office a second time with an almost unanimous electorate vote with only two states meekly dissenting.

Now observe how the Wheel of Life began to reverse itself and turn back in the other direction. The President changed his policy from definiteness of purpose to indefiniteness and drifting.

His change of policy split the powerful labor group and turned more than half of it against him. It split the almost-solid following he held in both houses of Congress, and more important than all this, it split the American people into "pro" and "anti" groups with the result that about all the President had left of his original political assets was his million-dollar smile and his ready handshake—obviously not enough to enable him to regain the power he once wielded in American life.

Here, then, we have an excellent example of a man who skyrocketed to great power through definiteness of purpose and bellyflopped to the starting point by his habit of drifting. In both his rise and his fall can be seen clearly the operation of the principles of drifting and non-drifting reaching a climax through the power of hypnotic rhythm and time.

All my life the Devil had a dramatic story to tell of his dealings with me. He saw me drift in and out of scores of business opportunities for which many would have given a king's ransom. He saw me drifting in my policy of relating myself to others, particularly in my lack of caution in business dealings.

The circumstance which saved me from fatal control of the law of hypnotic rhythm was the definiteness of purpose with which, at long last, I dedicated my entire life to the organization of a philosophy of individual achievement. I drifted at one time or another on all my minor whims and endeavors, but my drifting was offset by my major purpose, which was sufficient to restore my courage and start me once more in the quest of knowledge every time I was defeated in connection with my minor aims.

I learned something of the hazardous nature of the habit of drifting while engaged in analyzing more than 25,000 people in connection with the organization of the Law of Success. These analyses showed that only two out of every 100 have a definite major aim in life. The other 98 were caught by the habit of drifting. It seems more than a coincidence that my analyses clearly corroborated the Devil's claim that he controls 98 out of every 100 people because of their habit of drifting.

Looking back over my own career, I can see clearly that I could have avoided the majority of the temporary defeats with which I met if I had been definitely following a plan for the attainment of my major purpose in life.

From my experience in having analyzed the problems of more than 5,000 families, I know, definitely, that the majority of married people who get out of harmony with each other do so because of the accumulation of a great number of little circumstances in their married relationship which could have been cleared up and disposed of as they arose if there had been a definite policy to do so. They do not live their married life with definiteness of purpose.

So the story has gone, all back down the ages. The man with the most definite plan and purpose and the most power rides on to victory. The others scurry for cover and get crushed under the heels of those who are more determined.

The answer is not hard to find. There is no use looking toward high heaven for it. For my part I would prefer to seek the answer from the Devil, for he would tell me quickly enough that victory goes to the people who know what they want and are determined to have it. They have mastered the habit of drifting. They have definite policies, definite plans, and definite objectives. Their opposition, which may outnumber them very greatly, has no chance against them because the opposition has no plan, no purpose, no policy except that of drifting along, hoping that something may turn up to help them. In those three brief sentences you have the sum and the substance of the difference between success and failure, power and lack of it.

We come, now, near to the end of our visit through this book. If we were to try to state in one brief sentence the most important part of that which I have tried to convey through the book, it would be something like this:

One's dominating desires can be crystallized into their physical equivalents through definiteness of purpose backed by definiteness of plans, with the aid of nature's law of hypnotic rhythm and time!

There you have the positive phase of the philosophy of individual achievement I have tried to describe through this book, brought down to an irreducible minimum of brevity and simplicity. If you expand the philosophy for the purpose of adapting it to the circumstances of life, you find that it is as broad as life itself, that it covers all human relationships, all human thoughts, aims, and desires.

So here we are, at the end of the strangest of all the thousands of interviews I have had with the great and the near great, over a period of fifty years of labor, in my search for the truths of life that lead to happiness and economic security.

How strange, indeed, that after having had active cooperation from such men as Carnegie, Edison, and Ford, I should have been compelled, finally, to go to the Devil for a working knowledge of the greatest of all the principles uncovered in my quest for truth. How strange that I was forced to experience poverty and failure and adversity in a hundred forms before being given the privilege of understanding and using a law of nature which softens the thrust of these wicked weapons or wipes them out altogether. But the strangest of all this dramatic experience which life has provided me is the simplicity of the law through which, if I had understood it, I could have transmuted my desires into substantial form without having to undergo so many years of hardship and misery.

I find now, at the end of my interview with the Devil, that I had been carrying in my own pockets the matches with which the fires of adversity were being touched off. And I find, too, that the water with which those fires were finally extinguished was at my command in great abundance.

I searched for the philosopher's lodestone with which failure may be converted into success, only to learn that both success and failure are the results of day-to-day evolutionary forces through which dominating thoughts are pieced together bit by bit and woven into the things we want or the things we do not want, according to the nature of those thoughts.

How unfortunate that I did not understand this truth from the time that I reached the age of reason, for if I had understood it then I might have been able to go around some of the hurdles I have been forced to jump as I walked through "The Valley of the Shadow" of life.

The story of my interview with the Devil is now in your hands. The benefits you will receive from it will be in exact proportion to the thought it inspires in you. To benefit from reading the interview, you need not agree with every portion of it.

You have only to think and to reach your own conclusions concerning every part of it. How reasonable that is. You are the judge and the jury and the attorney for both the prosecution and the defense. If you do not win your case, the loss and the cause thereof will be yours!

—NAPOLEON HILL

The Secret Chapter

My Invisible Counselors

The author has for many years followed the habit of taking personal inventory of himself once a year, for the purpose of determining how many of his weaknesses he has bridged or eliminated, and to ascertain what progress, if any, he has made during the year.

On one of these occasions, before THE LAW OF SUCCESS philosophy had been reduced to textbooks and published, the inventory showed the author had not only slowed down during the year, but that he was becoming indifferent toward himself and toward life. He was scheduled to deliver an address in Ohio, some two hundred miles from his home. The trip was made by automobile.

On the way the author's "guardian angel" took her place beside him on the vacant front seat of the car. (This portion of the incident may, if the reader desires, be attributed entirely to the author's use of his imagination, or to daydreaming, or to any other cause one sees fit.)

The personage on the vacant seat beside the author seemed very real.

There took place, almost immediately after the author observed by his "feelings" that some force or personality beside his own was in the car, the following interview, which resulted in the Compact described:

Voice speaking to me from within: You have wasted more of your time in the past than you have used constructively. How long are you going to continue this waste?

The author: Yes, I know I have wasted too much time. What has been the cause of this waste, and how can I make amends for it in the future?

Voice from within: The time you have wasted in the main has been the time you have devoted to thinking and indulging too freely in physical pleasures. You should make amends for this waste by transmuting this vital energy into a service to others, through THE LAW OF SUCCESS philosophy.

The author: Do I understand that my thoughts in the future should be devoted entirely to serving others through the LAW OF SUCCESS?

Voice from within: Not at all, but you should divert the major portion of your thoughts to the purpose suggested. If you fail to do so, you will bring misery to yourself, and deprive others of knowledge which you should impart to them through the LAW OF SUCCESS.

The author: I haven't the money with which to publish the LAW OF SUCCESS philosophy.

Voice from within: That is no excuse. You may have all the money you need for this, and for every other purpose, provided you are willing to accept advice and follow it.

The author: I am willing to accept advice and I will follow it. Give me instructions, and I will follow them to the letter.

Voice from within: Very well, your willingness to follow instructions is all that you need for the present. Are you ready to receive your instructions?

The author: I am ready.

Voice from within: You will find it difficult at first to follow your instructions, because you will have to change completely your habits. The reward which awaits you, if you follow instructions faithfully, however, is worth all the effort you will devote to the task. Here are your instructions:

> **First.** In the future, you shall devote as much time and effort to serving others, through the LAW OF SUCCESS philosophy, as you have devoted in the past to indulgence in personal pleasures.
>
> **Second.** Proceed at once to the task of writing the LAW OF SUCCESS philosophy. When the manuscripts have been completed, you will receive further instructions for their publication.
>
> **Third.** Upon publication of the LAW OF SUCCESS, philosophy you will receive instructions for the writing of other books. Carry out those instructions as soon as you receive them.
>
> **Fourth.** As compensation for carrying out these and other instructions which will be given to you in the future, you may have your choice of any three things you wish.

The Author: Do you mean that I may really have any three things I choose, in return for carrying out these instructions?"

Voice from within: Yes, any three things you choose.

The Author: With whom am I dealing? Who will be responsible to me for the compensation I have been promised after I carry out the instructions?

Voice from within: You are dealing with Infinite Intelligence. I am the Individual Entity designated by Infinite Intelligence to bargain with you for your services. So you may proceed with your instructions with faith that you will receive your reward. I shall now give you the power to compensate yourself as soon as you earn your reward.

The Author: Very well. I shall choose (1) Wisdom through an understanding heart that will help me to relate myself to others in a spirit of harmony; (2) Health in both body and mind, and (3) Wealth in such amounts as I may need to carry out the instruction you have given me.

Voice from within: It is not enough. I cannot permit you to be cheated. You should modify your first choice to include happiness. Without happiness you will not be an efficient worker. Infinite Intelligence has selected you to assume a great responsibility. A world-crisis is impending. You have been prepared to render useful service in connection with this crisis. Revise your first choice.

The Author: All right! My first choice shall be happiness through the wisdom of an understanding heart.

Voice speaking from within: That is better! The terms of our compact are now satisfactory. You are now assuming the role of both master and servant. Your wages shall be paid as fast as the service is rendered. I shall explain the method by which you shall be paid, so that you will know you can neither collect without earning your pay, nor be cheated out of your reward after earning it.

Happiness comes only from rendering useful service to others. You shall receive this portion of your reward as fast as you earn it.

The wisdom of an understanding heart comes through intense desire for it. Take this portion of your reward as rapidly as you wish.

Health of body and mind comes through positive thought. Keep your mind free from negative thoughts and claim this portion of your reward as fast as you earn it.

Wealth of this sort, which will permit happiness, comes by rendering useful service to others. Through the LAW OF SUCCESS you may render such service. The money will be paid directly to you by those whom you serve, and in proportion to the amount of service you render, the quality of the service, and the number of people served.

Infinite Intelligence has very wisely made you your own supervisor, your own employer, your own servant, and your own paymaster. The compact is now in force. The extent to which it is carried out is limited only by you. This is irrevocable except by your own default.

My visitor departed, leaving behind a feeling of aloneness, similar to that which one might have felt if a fellow-traveler had opened the door of the car and stepped out. The experience was uncanny. I had never had such an experience before. For a time I was not sure what had happened.

Many thoughts ran through my mind. The first was that I had been daydreaming. Another was that I had been overworking my imagination. Subsequent events proved both thoughts to be wrong.

Briefly, the following, took place, after that experience on the twenty-sixth of October, 1923 (my birthday):

(a) Upon my return home the following day I began to organize the data I had been gathering on the LAW OF SUCCESS philosophy for nearly fifteen years previously On the following Christmas evening I began the actual writing of the LAW OF SUCCESS.

(b) Late in the year 1928 the manuscripts had been completed, after many revisions, and they were published by A. L. Felton of Meriden, Connecticut, through circumstances which fully harmonize with the terms of the compact already described.

(c) In 1929 the world-wide "Business Depression" began creating a state of chaos throughout the civilized world. Examination of the LAW OF SUCCESS philosophy will disclose the fact that it is perfectly suited to the needs of millions of people who have been injured by loss of faith, and in other ways by the depression.

(d) The LAW OF SUCCESS philosophy now has a following in all cities, towns and villages in America, and in practically every country on earth. The means of distribution of the philosophy (which I have described in other books recently written) came through media which harmonize perfectly with the terms of the compact.

(e) Last, but by no means least, I am healthy in both body and mind; I am happier than I have ever been before in my entire life, and I have not wanted for the money necessary to carry out my instructions.

The part of this experience which impresses me most is the ingenuity with which the compact was so designed that it gave me both the privilege of becoming the master, and the responsibility of being the servant. Literally, this compact made me the "Master of my own fate, the Captain of my own soul."

And right here is an appropriate place at which to call attention to a real benefit which anyone may experience by deliberately focusing attention upon any form of constructive desire. The mind acts upon one's dominating, or most pronounced desires. There is no escape from this fact. It is a fact indeed. "Be careful what you set your heart upon, for it surely shall be yours."

DID THEY SPEAK FROM THE GRAVE?

While I was passing through the age of "hero-worship" I found myself trying to imitate those whom I most admired. Moreover, I discovered that the element of faith, with which I endeavored to imitate my idols, gave me great capacity to do so quite successfully.

I have never quite divested myself of, this habit of hero worship, although I have passed the age commonly given over to such state of being. My experience has taught me that the next best thing to being truly great is to emulate the great, by feeling and action, as nearly as possible. I have never known of this habit doing anyone any harm.

Long before the LAW OF SUCCESS philosophy was completed, before I had ever written a line for publication or endeavored to deliver a speech in public, I followed the habit of reshaping my own character by trying to imitate the nine men whose lives and lifeworks had been most impressive to me. These nine men were Emerson, Paine, Edison, Darwin, Lincoln, Burbank, Napoleon, Ford and

Carnegie. Every night, over a long period of years, I held an imaginary council meeting with this group, whom I called my "Invisible Counselors."

The procedure was this: Just before going to sleep at night, I would shut my eyes and see, in my imagination, this group of men seated with me around my council table. Here I had not only an opportunity to sit among those whom I considered to be great, but I actually dominated the group by serving as the chairman and leader.

I had a very definite purpose in indulging my imagination through these nightly meetings. My purpose was to rebuild my own character so it would represent a composite of my imaginary counselors. Realizing, as I did early in life, that I had to overcome the handicap of a lowly birth in an environment of ignorance and superstition, I deliberately assigned myself the task of voluntary rebirth through the method here described.

STUDY GUIDE

The Secret Chapter: My Invisible Counselors

1. During his drive to Ohio, Napoleon Hill conversed through thoughts and feelings he was having, in a dialogue with a voice from within him (likening the voice as being an angel). He was told that he wasted too much time indulging in physical pleasures. Do you ever find yourself doing so to the point where it may affect your ability to focus on manifesting your desires?

2. He was told to make amends by transmuting his vital energy into a service to others through sharing the LAW OF SUCCESS philosophy in a book. He was then given instructions to follow. Focus on the greatest goal that you would like to achieve in your life. Then ask yourself if you can apply the following to that goal:
   - Devote as much time and effort toward serving others as you have devoted in the past toward indulgences in your personal pleasures.
   - Immediately take all necessary actions toward completing the task (in this case, Napoleon Hill to write the LAW OF SUCCESS philosophy).
   - Once your task is completed, you will receive other instructions that you must also follow as you get them.
   - To be compensated, in the future, you may have your choice of any three wishes. What would they be?

3. Napoleon's three wishes were (1) wisdom through an understanding heart that will help him to relate himself to others in a spirit of harmony; (2) health in both body and mind, and (3) wealth in such amounts as he may need to carry out the instructions that were given to him. He was told that his wishes were not enough and that he should choose happiness in his first wish. Did you consider and include happiness among your wishes?

4. The voice stated that "happiness comes only from rendering useful service to others." Do you believe this to be true? Provide evidence of it in your life.

5. The voice continued by stating that "the wisdom of an understanding heart comes through the intense desire for it." Do you have an intense desire for the three wishes that you listed? If not, consider revising them.

6. The money that Napoleon Hill was to receive for his services would be "in proportion to the amount of service he rendered, the quality of that service, and the number of people served." Rereading your wishes, do you believe that they sufficiently serve others in a manner that would match your desired compensation? If not, please consider revising them.

7. What delighted Napoleon Hill most about this exchange was that it gave him both the "privilege of becoming the master, and the responsibility of being the servant." Do you see a means by which following your heart's desire and the outcome you've chosen can serve you in a similar way? If so, how?

8. Napoleon worshipped many heroes in his life, and he very successfully imitated them. He shared that "the next best thing to being truly great is to emulate the great, by feeling and action, as nearly as possible." Do you currently have any heroes in your life? Have you ever tried to imitate them?

9. If you could rebuild your character so that you have all the attributes of those whom you admire most in your life, who would those individuals be and what traits do they possess that you would emulate? For example, I would have the compassion of Mother Teresa, I would have the wisdom and wealth of Warren Buffett, I would have the intelligence of Albert Einstein, I would have the oratorical prowess of Maya Angelou, I would have the charisma of Lady Diana, and so on.

10. Napoleon Hill reshaped his character by creating and emulating an imaginary council meeting of nine men that he most admired. Choose nine women and men that you admire most (they could be people that you know, famous people, business leaders, from anywhere in the world). If you want to act out their roles, do so. If not, close your eyes and imagine meeting with them. See them hearing you and supporting you. Allow yourself to feel into the connections with each of them, and experience a genuine spirit of integrity, generosity, and support. Try doing this before you go to sleep each night for five minutes, for a duration of two weeks. Then write about your experiences.

Rebuilding Character Through Auto-Suggestion

Having been an earnest student of psychology, I knew of course that all people become what they are because of their dominating thoughts and desires. I knew that every deeply seated desire may be transmuted into its physical counterpart. I knew that self-suggestion was a powerful factor in the building of character; that it was in fact the sole principle through which character is built!

With this knowledge of the principles of mind operation, I was fairly well armed with the equipment needed in rebuilding my character. In these imaginary council meetings, I called on my Cabinet members for the knowledge and the traits of character I wished each to contribute, addressing myself to each member, in audible words, as follows:

Mr. Emerson, I desire to acquire from you the marvelous understanding of Nature which distinguished your life. I ask that you make an impress upon my subconscious mind of whatever qualities you possessed which enabled you to understand and adapt yourself to the laws of Nature. I ask that you assist me in reaching and drawing upon whatever sources of knowledge are available to this end.

Mr. Burbank, I request that you pass on to me the knowledge which enabled you to so harmonize the laws of Nature that you caused the cactus to shed its thorns, and become an edible food. Give me access to the knowledge which enabled you to make two blades of grass grow where but one grew before, and helped you to blend the coloring of the flowers with more splendor and harmony. For you alone have successfully painted the lily.

Napoleon, I desire to acquire from you, by emulation the marvelous ability you possessed to inspire men and to arouse them to a greater and more determined spirit of action. Also to acquire the spirit of enduring faith which enabled you to turn defeat into victory, and to surmount staggering obstacles. Emperor of Fate, King of Chance, Man of Destiny, I salute you!

Mr. Paine, I desire to acquire from you the freedom of your thought and the courage and clarity with which to express your convictions, which so distinguished you!

Mr. Darwin, I wish to acquire from you the marvelous patience and ability to study cause and effect, without bias or prejudice, so exemplified by you in the field of natural science.

Mr. Lincoln, I desire to build into my own character the keen sense of justice, the untiring spirit of patience, the sense of humor, the spirit of human understanding and the tolerance which were your distinguishing characteristics.

Mr. Carnegie, I am already indebted to you for my choice of a life-work, which has brought me great happiness and peace of mind. I wish to acquire a thorough understanding of the principles of organized effort which you used so effectively in the building of a great industrial enterprise.

Mr. Ford, you have been among the most helpful of the men who have supplied much of the material out of which the philosophy of achievement is being built. I wish to acquire your spirit of persistence, your determination, your poise, and your self-confidence, with which you have mastered poverty, organized directness, unified and simplified human effort, so I may help others to follow in your footsteps.

Mr. Edison, I have seated you nearest to me, at my right, because of the personal cooperation you have given me during my research into the causes of success and failure. I wish to acquire from you the marvelous spirit of faith with which you have uncovered so many of Nature's secrets, and the spirit of unremitting toil with which you have so often wrested victory from defeat."

My method of addressing the members of my imaginary Cabinet would vary, according to the traits of character in which I was, for the moment, most interested in acquiring. I studied the records of their lives with painstaking care. After some three months of this sort of nightly procedure, I was astounded by the discovery that these imaginary figures became apparently real.

Each of these nine men developed individual characteristics which surprised me. For example, Lincoln developed the habit of being always late, then walking around the table in a solemn parade. When he came he walked very slowly, with his hands clasped behind him, and once in a while, he would stop at my seat as he passed and rest his hand momentarily, upon my shoulder. He always wore an expression of seriousness upon his face. Rarely did I see him smile. The cares of a sundered nation had made him grave.

That was not true of the others. Burbank and Paine often indulged in witty repartee which seemed at times to shock the other members of my Cabinet.

One night Paine suggested that I prepare a lecture on "The Age of Reason," and deliver it from the pulpit of a church which

I formerly attended. Many around the table laughed heartily at the suggestion. But Napoleon did not. He drew his mouth down at the corners and groaned so loudly that they all turned and looked at him with amazement. To him the church was but a pawn of the State, not to be reformed, but to be used, as a convenient inciter to mass activity by the people.

On one occasion Burbank was late. When he came he was excited with enthusiasm, and explained that he had been delayed because of an experiment he was making, through which he hoped to be able to grow apples on most any sort of tree.

Paine chided him by reminding him that it was an apple which started all the trouble between man and woman.

Darwin chuckled heartily as he suggested that Paine should watch out for little serpents when he went out into the forest to gather apples, as they had the habit of growing into big snakes.

Emerson observed, "No serpents, no apples." And Napoleon remarked, "No apples, no state!"

Once I had a love affair with a young lady whose name was Josephine. We had a misunderstanding and agreed to discontinue our love affair. That evening at the meeting Napoleon smiled as he reminded me that he too had given up a cherished possession whose name was Josephine, and admonished me to re-establish myself in the young lady's good graces. I did not follow the advice.

Years later I met the young lady, after she had married another man, and she told me that shortly after she and I had our break, she had a dream in which Napoleon appeared and strongly urged her to recant, and invite me to do the same.

Lincoln developed the habit of being always the last one to leave the table after each meeting. On one occasion, he leaned across the end of the table on his folded arms, and remained in that position for several minutes. I made no attempt to disturb him.

Finally he lifted his head slowly, got up and walked to the door, then turned around, came back, and laid his hand on my shoulder and said, "My boy, you will need much courage if you remain steadfast in carrying out your purpose in life. But remember, when difficulties overtake that the common people have common sense. Adversity will develop it."

One evening Edison arrived ahead of all the others. He seated himself at my left, where Emerson was accustomed to sit.

Edison, you are destined to witness the discovery of the secret of life. When the time comes you will observe that life consists of great swarms of energy, or entities, each as intelligent as human beings believe themselves to be.

These units of life group themselves together like hives of bees, and remain together until they disintegrate through lack of harmony. These units have differences of opinion, just as do human beings, and often they fight among themselves.

These meetings which you are conducting will be very helpful to you. They will bring to your rescue some of the same units of life which served the members of your Cabinet, whose physical bodies have been discarded. These units are eternal. They never die!

Your own thoughts and desires serve as the magnet which attracts units of life from the great ocean of life. Only the friendly units which harmonize with the nature of your desires are attracted.

The other members of the Cabinet began to enter the room. Edison rose and slowly walked around to his own seat. Edison was still living when this happened. It impressed me so greatly that I went to see him and told him about the experience. He smiled broadly, and said: "Your dream was more a reality than you may imagine it to have been." He added no further explanation to his statement.

These meetings became so realistic that I became fearful of their consequence, and discontinued them for several months. The experiences were so uncanny that I was afraid my mind might become unbalanced if I continued them, or that I would become a fanatic on the subject and lose sight of the fact that these meetings were purely experiences of my imagination.

Some six months after I had discontinued the practice I was awakened one night, or thought I was, when I saw Lincoln standing at my bedside. He said, "The world will soon need your services. It is about to undergo a period of chaos which will cause men and women to lose faith and become panic stricken. Go ahead with your work and complete your philosophy. That is your mission in life. If you neglect it, for any cause whatsoever, you will be reduced to a primal state and be compelled to retrace the cycles through which you have passed during thousands of years."

I was unable to tell when morning came whether I had dreamed this, or had actually been awake, and I have never since found out which it was, but I do know that the dream—if it were a dream—was so vivid in my mind the next day that I resumed my meetings the following night and have ever since continued them.

At our next meeting the members of my Cabinet all filed into the room together and stood at their accustomed places at the council table, while Lincoln raised a glass and said, "Gentlemen, let us drink a toast to a friend of man. He has returned to the fold."

After that I began to add new members to my Cabinet, until now it consists of more than fifty, among them Galileo, Copernicus, Aristotle, Plato,

Socrates, Homer, Voltaire, Bruno, Spinoza, Drummond, Kant, Schopenhauer, Newton, Confucius, Elbert Hubbard, Brann, Ingersoll, Wilson and William James.

This is the first time that I have had the courage to mention this chapter of my life. Heretofore, I have remained quiet on the subject because I knew, from my own attitude in connection with such matters, that I would be branded as a pious fraud if I described my unusual experiences.

I have been emboldened by time to reduce my experiences to the printed page because the philosophy of achievement which I have had the privilege of organizing has been accepted as being sound and practical by a great army of men and women in practically every walk of life.

Also I am now less concerned about what "they will say" than I was in the past. One of the blessings of maturity is that it sometimes brings one greater courage to be truthful, regardless of what those who do not understand may think or say.

Lest I be misunderstood, I wish here to state most emphatically that I still regard my Cabinet meetings as being purely imaginary, but I feel entitled to suggest that, while the members of my Cabinet may be purely fictional, and the meetings entirely existent in my own imagination, they have led me into glorious paths of adventure, rekindled an appreciation of true greatness, encouraged creative endeavor, and emboldened the expression of honest thought.

STUDY GUIDE

Rebuilding Character through Auto-Suggestion

1. Following Napoleon Hill's guidance, have a dialogue with each of your nine mentors, requesting what specific attributes you wish from each. For example, in his conversation with Emerson, he asks, "Mr. Emerson, I desire to acquire from you the marvelous understanding of Nature which distinguished your life. I ask that you make an impress upon my subconscious mind of whatever qualities you possessed which enabled you to understand and adapt yourself to the laws of Nature. I ask that you assist me in reaching and drawing upon whatever sources of knowledge are available to this end." Ask each of them to impress upon your conscious and subconscious mind all that you wish to learn from them. Then be sure to write about your experiences with each.

2. If you find this exercise useful, continue to do it prior to going to bed, and continue writing about any insights or experiences you have in response to it.

After doing this exercise for three months, Napoleon Hill started to experience each member of his imaginary cabinet as real. He shared stories of some exceptional and vivid experiences. While he was reluctant to write about his experiences with the cabinet members, in the end he did so.

Do you consider his experiences to be truth or fiction? Either way, stories were shared, advice was given, most likely energy frequency was raised, all within the spirit of definiteness of purpose, most likely developed into a hypnotic rhythm in his life that supported him in growing wiser and more successful with the passage of time.

www.ingramcontent.com/pod-product-compliance
Ingram Content Group UK Ltd.
Pitfield, Milton Keynes, MK11 3LW, UK
UKHW021516040125
453159UK00023B/314